Latin America and the World Economy

CANADA

UNITED STATES

ATLANTIC OCEAN

Gulf of Mexico

THE BAHAMAS
CUBA
HAITI
DOMINICAN REPUBLIC
PUERTO RICO (U.S.)

MEXICO

BELIZE
JAMAICA
Caribbean Sea

BARBADOS
GRENADA
TRINIDAD & TOBAGO
GUYANA
SURINAME
FRENCH GUIANA (France)

GUATEMALA
HONDURAS
EL SALVADOR
NICARAGUA
COSTA RICA
PANAMA

VENEZUELA

COLOMBIA

ECUADOR

PERU

BRAZIL

PACIFIC OCEAN

BOLIVIA

PARAGUAY

CHILE

ARGENTINA

URUGUAY

N
W E
S

0   600   1200 miles

0   600   1200 kilometers

Latin America

PROBLEMS IN WORLD HISTORY

Latin America and the World Economy

Dependency and Beyond

Richard J. Salvucci

Trinity University

D. C. Heath and Company
Lexington, Massachusetts   Toronto

Address editorial correspondence to:
D. C. Heath and Company
125 Spring Street
Lexington, MA 02173

Acquisitions: James Miller
Development: Pat Wakeley
Editorial Production: Celena Sun
Design: Henry Rachlin
Art Editing: Gary Crespo
Cover Photo Research: Pembroke Herbert and Sandi Rygiel/Picture
   Research Consultants
Production Coordination: Michael O'Dea
Permissions: Margaret Roll

Published simultaneously in Canada.

Printed in the United States of America.

International Standard Book Number: 0-669-35174-1

Library of Congress Catalog Number: 95-78794

10 9 8 7 6 5 4 3 2

For Martin and Rosie, My Buddies

Preface

The edited readings collected here have proved useful to me in teaching an undergraduate course on the economic history of Latin America. The readings represent a variety of disciplinary, methodological, and ideological perspectives. They range widely over time and place and convey something of the breadth of the existing literature. Some are explicitly critical of dependency and world systems analyses, although most are really "post-dependency" in outlook. The readings offer no simplistic celebrations of free markets or of the religion of competition. Even those selections deeply informed by "mainstream" economic thinking offer thoughtful reflections on what Latin Americans call neoliberalism, essentially a reliance on the private sector and unimpeded market forces to produce growth and development. Yet the readings also generally share a commitment to empiricism and, in that sense, reject the "theoretical" or, put more accurately, speculative cast of much dependency and world-systems thinking. Although much of the original statistical analysis has been omitted for the sake of simplicity, those who examine the original articles, papers, chapters, and essays will find that they marshal an impressive volume of quantitative research. To repeat, the readings collected here are nothing if not empirically oriented.

As in other volumes in the Problems in World History series, virtually every reading in this anthology is "historical" in the sense of emphasizing the past rather than the present. Yet many selections address contemporary concerns and draw on historical data for illumination—for "lessons" from the past. Good historical writing is by no means the exclusive domain of historians. Here one finds contributions by both economists and historians, many informed by studies of international political economy. A number of scholars represented here have also suggested ways of discussing their work, as indicated in the introductions to specific selections. Paul Gootenberg, Stephen Haber, Robert Patch, and Enrique Semo were especially generous with their time.

I am also grateful to those who reviewed the outline for this volume and offered valuable suggestions: Carmen Diana Deere, University of Massachusetts, Amherst; Erwin P. Grieshaber, Mankato State University; June E. Hahner, SUNY, Albany; Lyman L. Johnson, University of North Carolina, Charlotte; and Paul J. Vanderwood, San Diego State University. To all of them, my thanks.

This anthology was assembled as a financial crisis shook Mexico in late 1994 and threatened to destabilize the other major economies of the region as well. Several months later, unemployment remained high in Argentina and Mexico, even as experts debated the implications of the most recent crisis. Yet other parts of Latin America were seemingly unaffected, as the experience of Chile, Colombia, and Peru demonstrated. Still, it is generally true that the economies of Latin America are more open to international trade and finance today than at any other time since the early twentieth century. A historical approach, then, seems particularly relevant to resolving the uncertainties of the moment by drawing on the experiences of the past, for little that we see is utterly unprecedented. Hence the purpose of this small volume.

R.J.S.

CONTENTS

Introduction

This volume presents a selective survey of views regarding the relation of Latin America to the international economy from the sixteenth century to the present. Admittedly, none of the selections advocates commercial or financial isolation, an outlook that the late Carlos Díaz Alejandro once characterized as "unhinged." All, however, draw subtle, challenging, and sometimes unexpected conclusions from the evidence they weigh. The readings on the colonial period, for example, view international trade as more than just a means by which Spain and Portugal, or other European powers, extracted a surplus from their colonies. Trade was instead a means of colonial capital accumulation or a mechanism that knit together otherwise separate markets. And the readings emphasize that domestic production and internal markets cannot be arbitrarily isolated from the foreign sector. Historians may justifiably reject the exaggerated emphasis that dependency thinking and world-systems analysis put on international trade and capital flows, but they realize that it is equally misleading to neglect the influence of trade and investment entirely. For instance, an emerging post-dependency school argues that the native peoples of the Americas shaped the ways in which commercial integration took place, or were themselves often active beneficiaries of this integration. Moreover, the direct resource transfers that trade produced sometimes affected the economies of the new world more than those of the old. Or the impact of trade was greatest on those activities whose productivity was highest, but whose share of overall economic activity was not inevitably greatest. Simple notions of unequal trade or dependent development hardly do justice to the actual complexity of commercial development.

The readings on the nineteenth century draw attention to the often limited, hesitant, and piecemeal integration of the former colonies of Spain and Portugal into the Atlantic economy. Where commercialization was most advanced, economic theory offers stimulating and elegant explanations of the resulting patterns of development. Yet there were also cases in which political, cultural, and geographical constraints prevented fuller international integration until the century was well advanced. The cosmopolitan elites who advocated the importance of commercial liberalism were often opposed by a variety of domestic groups. In some cases, these "backward" interests proved difficult to overcome. The rise and fall of their influence was by no means uniform, linear, or simply described. Historians know that the idea of "Latin America" was an invention of the nineteenth century, but even so, use of the term can obscure a considerable diversity of experience. Moreover, countries with restricted access to international markets often had an acute appreciation of the costs of isolation. For example, the correspondence of Mexican ministers who wrestled with the problem of sovereign debt in the late 1820s and 1830s reveals a deeper understanding of its implications than some of the historians who have examined the issue.

Finally, the readings that deal with the twentieth century explain Latin America's retreat from the flood tide of international economic integration at the end of the nineteenth century, and they do so with remarkable understanding. None are so naive as to dismiss the inward–looking policies of the post–World War II era as nothing more than misguided "failures." Instead, they point to high and sustained rates of economic growth, substantial (if uneven) social development, and to the often changing political imperatives on which such policies were based. It is sometimes easy to forget policies that today are targets for reform were another decade's "miracles." History suggests that the "pathways from the periphery" are indeed diverse. If anything, the readings emphasize that dogmatism is inappropriate and that the shelf life of many policy prescriptions turns out to be quite limited.

Although several of the edited readings that follow are very well known and a few are classics, others draw on more specific cases or on historical episodes that are less familiar. Yet all share the conviction that understanding the international economy is critical for fully understanding the historical evolution of the Latin American economies.

PART I

Core and Periphery?
Colonial Beginnings

Modern views of colonial Latin America and the international econ-omy reflect a variety of perspectives and concerns. In a sense, the fa-miliar concepts of dependency and unequal exchange are merely ways in which the historian makes sense of the economic impact of imperialism and colonialism. As long ago as 1947, Clarence Haring wrote in *The Spanish Empire in America* that Castilian mercantil-ism "was essentially a protectionist system . . . aimed largely at ex-port commerce." Export commerce, in turn, supported metropoli-tan military and naval power and the accumulation of wealth through a favorable balance of trade. In Haring's view, trade, power, and the colonial system depended on "a rigid and elaborate commercial [structure] through whose operation a larger part of the wealth of America might ultimately be syphoned [*sic*] back to Spain."

Haring never used the term *dependency*, which gained currency well after he wrote. Stanley Stein and his wife, Barbara Hadley Stein, would adapt and extend Haring's insight in their widely read and very influential work, *The Colonial Heritage of Latin America: Essays on Economic Dependence in Perspective* (1970). As the Steins wrote, "[M]etropolitan Spain fell back upon an essentially late medieval commercial system, a sort of mercantilism . . . to profit from its American possessions. . . . The system acquired con-trol over . . . mining . . . and a monopoly of distribution. . . . The export orientation of the Latin American economy . . . was a prod-uct of the first two hundred years of Spanish colonialism. . . . " This external orientation was seen, on balance, as an impediment to ra-tional economic growth, for it reflected Spain's desire to shape the economies of its American possessions in ways intended solely to maximize metropolitan power and wealth. As Guillermo Céspedes wrote in *América Hispánica (1492–1898)* (1983), America at the time of the Conquest "aspired to [economic] diversification and self-sufficiency [that would have permitted] a slow but balanced development." But through the agency of colonialism, "[America] was transformed into a modern economy, specialized and capitalist, unbalanced in favor of mining and export to Europe. This new economic *dependency* (italics added) . . . that would last for centuries, is the origin of the modern 'underdevelopment' of certain Iberoamerican regions, which is the result of an intense but nevertheless unbalanced reliance on external demand." Or to quote from the famous opening sentences of André Gunder Frank's *Capitalism and Underdevelopment in Latin America* (1967), "My thesis is that [capitalism] and the historical development of the capitalist system have generated underdevelopment in the peripheral satellites whose economic surplus was expropriated [through the export of raw materials and the import of manufactures], while generating economic development in the metropolitan centers which appropriated that surplus. . . . "

All this scholarly emphasis on the external sector—on international trade and capital movements—produced an inevitable reaction. Frank's writings in particular invited critical scrutiny because of their transparent theoretical and analytical weaknesses. Yet the interests of working historians were evolving. A competing focus on internal production, consumption, and exchange had been evident at least since the publication of Woodrow Borah's *New Spain's Century of Depression* (1951). In the 1970s and 1980s, an important series of works by diverse scholars, including Peter Bakewell's *Silver Mining and Society in Colonial Mexico* (1971) and Carlos Sempat Assadourian's *El sistema de la economía colonial: mercado interno, regiones y espacio económico* (1982) appeared. They focused on internal colonial markets because those markets were larger and because most goods used in everyday life—the classic triad of food, clothing, and shelter—were produced and consumed within the colonies themselves. Implicitly, then, historians were saying that the ratio of foreign trade to domestic production was small, as was the ratio of net capital flows (that is, flows of savings in and out of the colonies) to total investment.

The clearest expression of these themes and of their broader political and social implications was John Lynch's *The Spanish Ameri-*

can Revolution, 1808–1826 (1973). The commercial opening of Latin America was no longer thought to have occurred during the first conquest, as Frank had argued. Instead, historians increasingly believed that Spanish America, at least, had come to depend mostly on its own resources by the beginning of the seventeenth century, if not before. It was not until late in the day, in the eighteenth century, that the "Bourbon reconquest," in the words of British historian David Brading, reoriented the focus of colonial production—at least in the sense that trade and capital movements had a substantial impact on promoting or retarding economic growth. Even the Spanish possessions in the Caribbean, such as Cuba and Puerto Rico, began their modern careers as export economies in the eighteenth or early nineteenth century. Previous sugar booms, and their intensive relation to international trade and finance had been the province of Portuguese Brazil beginning in the 1570s, and by the middle of the seventeenth century, of the English and French possessions in the Caribbean, such as Barbados, Jamaica, and Saint-Domingue. And yet even in Brazil, where sugar plantations had taken root along the northeastern coast by the 1580s, the production of foodstuffs such as manioc was at least partially the domain of peasant cultivators. Economic development is at bottom a commercial story, but historians of colonial Latin America are now accustomed to casting a rather wider net.

Writers in the dependency tradition examined the impact of the international economy on colonial Latin America, but others were more interested in Latin America's contribution to the development of the world economy. One important school of thought is embodied in the widely discussed work of Immanuel Wallerstein, in particular his *The Modern World System: Capitalist Agriculture and the Origins of the European World-Economy in the Sixteenth Century* (1974). Wallerstein viewed the rise of early modern capitalism as a response to the crisis of European feudalism that occurred between 1300 and 1450. Integral to capitalism's rise was the creation of a world economy, as well as an international division of labor within it. In Wallerstein's view, the "periphery" (which included Latin America) produced the foodstuffs, raw materials, and labor that sustained those "core" states that ultimately became industrial nations: "[T]hose who breed manpower sustain those who grow food who sustain those who grow other raw materials who sustain those involved in industrial production." Moreover, unfree labor in the periphery supported free labor in the core. What Wallerstein calls "coerced cash crop labor," or "agricultural labor . . . where the peasants are required . . . to labor at least part of the time on a large domain producing some product for sale on the world market" was introduced to Latin America as a result of conquest. For Wallerstein, forced labor in colonial Latin America (and, as he describes, Eastern Europe) provided the rents and profits—the capital, in other words—on which the development and expansion of a free labor economy in Western Europe was based.

The readings that follow include some of the many responses to both dependency and world-system writing. The selections by Enrique Semo and Robert Patch address several aspects of dependency writing. Both suggest that the connection between trade and economic change in colonial Latin America was complex and by no means unambiguous. The impact of trade was neither all-pervasive nor uniformly negative. The selections by Patrick O'Brien and Stanley Lebergott take issue with a particular concern of world-system writing: to what extent did the resources of the periphery finance the development of the core?

Capitalism and Trade
in Early Mexico

ENRIQUE SEMO

Enrique Semo, a prominent Mexican intellectual, is known not only for his historical scholarship, but for his contributions to political journalism as well. His *History of Capitalism in Mexico,* which first appeared in 1973, captures Semo's complex understanding of the nature of dependency. Capitalism required more than two centuries to reach its fullest development in colonial Mexico. In the sixteenth and seventeenth centuries, Semo argues, the colonial elite was sustained by its ability to extract a surplus from the indigenous communities. Domestic production was lim-

Enrique Semo, *The History of Capitalism in Mexico: Its Origins, 1521–1763,* translated by Lidia Lozano, 1993, pp. 52–55, 61–64. Reprinted by permission of the University of Texas Press.

ited. Plunder and the spoils of conquest were the fundamental source of the Europeans' "primitive accumulation." By primitive accumulation, Semo means the surplus profits that were to be invested in domestic agriculture, commerce, manufacturing, mining, and trade. These activities Semo identifies as the nucleus of an expanding capitalist economy characterized by the use of generally free labor, by the accumulation of productive assets, and by largely market exchange. The evolution of colonial capitalism, in other words, was inseparable from the evolution of a colonial market. Only an expanding market could provide businesses with the incentives to innovate, to expand production, and to reduce costs. Semo identifies international trade as a possible source of capitalist development, because the international market was large and expanding. Of the industries in colonial Mexico linked to the international market, silver mining was the most important. Thus Semo suggests that both trade and mining played major roles in the creation of colonial capitalism. Silver mining could link Mexico's small and fragmented domestic markets together precisely because mining faced a large international demand. In this sense, Semo's positive assessment of the role of trade in economic development represents a less orthodox strand of dependency thinking.

Semo's belief that trade between Mexico and Spain was fundamentally unequal and exploitative is more conventional. The constant drain of silver from Mexico produced episodes of stagnating commerce as domestic Mexican demand fell. And Spain's position as a monopoly seller of goods in the Mexican market led to excess profits for Spanish merchants and growing revenues for the Spanish Crown. Yet Semo denies that commercial policy toward Mexico was excessively rigid. Spanish "mercantilism" was somewhat ineffectual. Semo points to the continued survival of textile manufacturing in colonial Mexico to make his point. Despite demands for the suppression of this industry by groups in Spain, nothing of the sort ever occurred.

Thus Semo's position on the impact of international trade on the colonial Mexican economy is ambiguous. Trade drove the expansion of silver mining in Mexico, and silver mining helped create a broader internal market for colonial producers. But trade was also unequal and transferred profits (and hence savings) from the Mexican colony to Spain. Semo thus shares the dependency notion that international trade produced a drain of capital from Spain's colonies. Yet he also allows that international trade can raise domestic productivity and income.

Spain Was "the Indies" of Other European Countries

For three hundred years, New Spain was a Spanish colony. However, since the sixteenth century, it had maintained an economic relationship of colonial exploitation with Europe's capitalist centers. This was made possible by the fact that, very early on, Spain had been reduced to the condition of a *country economically dependent* on other powers, whose capitalism was more advanced.

From an economic point of view, Spaniards played the role, largely, of middlemen. From the late sixteenth century, a network of channels had been consolidated. It originated in the most developed capitalist centers, passed through the "colonial powers" (Spain and Portugal), and ended in the American colonies. These channels served to extract the surplus product of colonial societies and to transform the latter into captive markets for French, English, Dutch, and even Italian manufactured goods.

German financiers plundered the Spanish Royal Treasury, and foreigners in Seville seized the lion's share of private profits. Very early, England began to assert its economic hold over the Iberian countries and, through them, over their colonies. In exchange for sea protection, English traders forced their entry into the Portuguese redoubt in the colonies of Africa, Asia, and Latin America. In the early seventeenth century, half of all textile exports from London went to Spain. A century later, English merchants had so many business interests in Spain and its colonies that, no sooner had Louis XIV of France's plans been made public to demand both the opening up of the Spanish colonies to French traders and the exclusion of the English, than Great Britain wholeheartedly embarked upon the Spanish wars of succession (1701–1713).

The surplus from America, which arrived in the metropolis in the form of silver, did not remain long in Spain. There were frequent complaints in the Spanish *cortes* about bullion leaving the country, and Spain was said to be "the Indies of other countries." Spain was primarily an exporter of raw materials and an importer of manufactured goods, with a negative balance of trade, whose deficit it met with American silver. Precious metals were taken out of the country illegally by Spanish merchants and foreign residents in Spain and channeled toward the large capitalist centers of production.

In a sense, precious metals were the crutches which enabled the Spanish economy to move. But on top of such clandestine exports, the state had to authorize legal payments in kind to import necessary food products and naval implements which had to be paid for in money. However, the larger payments were those made by the Crown in order to meet its commitments abroad . . . All roads taking precious metals out of the country converged in northern Europe, either directly from Bilbao or via France and Italy, since it was there that Spanish interests were liable and the balance of trade was worse. Money was crucial both for the conflict with France and the war against the Low Countries as well as for its relationship with northern Europe's economy, since it went via Amsterdam to Germany and to England, which also profited from the smuggling of bullion by Spanish traders in wool ships.[1]

Spanish production, which was not competitive at home, was even less capable of meeting the needs of the colonies. José Campillo y Cosío complained in 1740 that less than one-twentieth of the products used in the West Indies were of Spanish origin.

There were other European centers to turn to, and Spanish traders became genuine middlemen, not between Spanish producers and colonial consumers but between the latter and foreign producers, who were legally excluded from trading with the colonies.

Seville's merchants did not turn America into a monopoly market for Spanish goods, but they did so for products from other countries. New Spain became a major market, particularly for English and French textiles. Since the sixteenth century, European textiles accounted for three-quarters of all imports to New Spain. At the same time, the export of dyes for the textile industry grew in importance.

In the mid-eighteenth century, a representative for the big Spanish merchants described in the following terms the significance of Spanish trade to the rest of Europe: "[Spain's] trade has supplied many items for the wealth of the other nations, it feeds, drives and sustains their industry in a twofold way, with many raw materials essential to their manufactures and with a substantial amount of money with which every year it settles a balance favorable to its general trade in European industrial goods."

---

[1]John Lynch, *Spain Under the Hapsburgs* (Oxford: Blackwell's, 1964), 1:124–125.

On the other hand, illegal trading between European nations and Spain's American possessions grew considerably. Foreign merchants carried out such trading directly through Seville or Cádiz. They unloaded goods from their ships and loaded them straight onto Spanish vessels without signing the register of the Casa de Contratación, or, as early as the seventeenth century, they would simply call at colonial ports in their own ships. A sizable fleet, financed by Dutch, French, and English traders, was used for these activities with the consent of the colonies' inhabitants.

The wars waged by Spain in the mid-seventeenth century made transatlantic sailing particularly unsafe for Spanish ships. Fleets became more irregular. Between 1650 and 1770, Spain experienced only eighteen years of peace. At the beginning of this period, fleets would depart for Peru once a year. Later, they sailed every three, even four, years. After 1682, they did so every five or six years. As a result, contraband trade between Europe and the major Latin American centers increased substantially, and a significant proportion of the silver produced went—without prior payment of the *quinto* (the "fifth")—to pay for illegally imported commodities.

In the middle of the eighteenth century, C. H. Haring relates, "Don Bernardo de Uloa estimates contraband trade amounts to half the Cádiz trade. He bases this estimate on the number of ships which sail between Spain and America, which comes to no more than forty a year, whereas the English and the Dutch deploy more than 300 ships to sail to America via Curazao and Jamaica . . . The English admit that none of their colonies is as valuable to England as Jamaica, due to the contraband trade with Spaniards, and that the riches from this trade have made its inhabitants neglect their fields."

According to Kossok and Markow, "90% of colonial trade was directly or indirectly in foreign hands; more than 95% of American silver left the country [Spain] through contraband, through foreign trade deficit and through the servicing of foreign debts."

Chaunu has estimated that during the period 1561–1650, Spain obtained gains from its trade with Latin America four times greater than the value of goods exported. But Spanish traders acted only as commission agents, and the greater share of their colonial profits ended up in the capitalist centers of Holland, France, and England. The Spanish Empire imposed its major institutions on the colonies, but its role in their commercial exploitation was that of an increasingly weaker partner.

Taking these factors into account, we can speak of a degree of continuity in the economic status of Latin American countries from the sixteenth century to the present day. Despite changes in the forms of exploitation, their condition has been that of *countries directly or indirectly dependent on the more developed capitalist centers.* As a result, processes of surplus extraction, of decapitalization, of hypertrophy of export sectors, and of obstruction of industrial development have been at work for four centuries. These phenomena have been part of the global process of the rise and development of capitalism from its very first stages right through to its imperialist phase. Its economic essence is a relation that produces superprofits for the metropolis, be it through the monopoly control of trade or through the investment of capital that yields higher returns than those prevailing in the colonialist country.

The metropolis-colony relationship is present at every stage of development of the socioeconomic formation of all Latin American countries; it thus becomes *a constant* in their history, but not *their history,* as some historians and economists, who underestimate or deny the significance of internal factors, and who reduce complex historical development to the simplified metropolis-colony dichotomy, would claim. . . .

Fiscal Policy and Trade

Throughout the period under consideration, colonial exploitation of America made use of various channels. The ancient system of pillage and plundering prevailed during the Conquest. However, as relations became more stable, it was replaced by economic mechanisms such as the imposition of forced tributes and loans, the removal of wealth and capital by Spaniards returning home, and unequal trade. These mechanisms gave rise to a constant drain of precious metals, which was acutely felt with the departure of each fleet or ship from New Spain. The loss of silver and gold then was such that trade in the capital came to a halt for as long as three months after the boat's departure.

Feudal elements prevailed in some of these methods of exploitation. In others, on the other hand, the capitalist links of colonial exploitation—which would become established and would persist even after the Latin American countries became independent—burgeoned. Two extreme cases can be cited as examples: the Crown's fiscal system, in which the solid precapitalist elements of the Spanish empire were clearly manifested, and colonial trade, many of whose mechanisms of exploitation remain to this day.

Economically speaking, the Crown had only one interest in America: to obtain the necessary silver to finance the exorbitant expenses imposed by the empire. Through a complex system of royalties, tributes, taxes, monopolies, and forced loans, the Crown managed to retain a substantial share of colonial loot. Chapman has estimated that its American colonies yielded, roughly, some 70,000 pesos a year up to 1518, a total of 1.2 million up to 1554. After the conquest of Peru, the annual income rose to 3.5 million and reached 45 million during Philip II's reign; subsequently, it dropped, remaining at an average of 17 million throughout the century. Crown revenues grew rapidly. During the reign of Charles V, the budget tripled; during Philip II's, it quadrupled. Nevertheless, expenditure rose faster. Philip II inherited from his father a debt of 20 million ducats, and passed on to his successor one that was five times greater; numerous public loans, the two suspension-of-payment decrees in 1575 and 1596, respectively, and desperate financial moves document the endless voracity of the royal treasury and its growing indebtedness.

The fiscal system devised by the Crown to obtain revenues was governed by strictly feudal criteria, according to which all known production or income had to be taxed. There is a marked difference between the Spanish fiscal system and the English, which from the seventeenth century was designed to meet the needs of the commercial and manufacturing strata. The Spanish system of customs and monopolies was not fundamentally different from the systematic pillage carried out by feudal lords, who taxed everything from traveling on roads to opening windows . . .

In the beginning, the Crown actually attempted to keep sole monopoly over colonial trade, excluding all private individuals. The instructions given to Columbus in 1493 strictly forbade private individuals from trading directly with the Indies, and it was ordered that local transactions take place before a treasurer, a bookkeeper, and Columbus's representative. The colonizers were allowed to import from Spain whatever cattle and foodstuff were necessary for their survival, but none for trade purposes. They were expressly banned from introducing clothing, shoes, horses, and other items the trading of which was reserved for the Crown.

These measures, which revealed the weakness of commercial sectors during the early stage of the Conquest, were abandoned only when, as colonization spread, they became a clear obstacle, a source of permanent friction with merchants and *colonos* who demanded to share directly in the gains from the discovery and colonization. However, they were replaced by a limited monopoly, subject to considerable fiscal burdens, which benefited only the Crown and a few Seville and Cádiz trading houses.

Under monopoly regulations, colonial trade yielded substantially higher profits than those governing the exchange between countries of similar levels of development. There were huge differences between the sale price of products in their country of origin and in the American colonies. Since fleets were the only legal means of commercial traffic, the differences between the value of shipments transported by them to the metropolis and the value of merchandise taken back can be taken as an index of the unequal terms of trade.

> Normally the mainland fleets carried a value of eight, ten or twelve million pesos in European merchandise of all kinds; and these fleets came back in exchange with thirty or forty million pesos in gold, silver, vicuña wool, cacao and precious fruits from those kingdoms . . . sometimes the dealers made up to five hundred percent profits from merchandise of the lowest price and quality; but the common and sure gain from these trips was one hundred per cent.

Eighteenth-century Spanish economists knew very well that those mercantilist principles according to which the wealth of a country lies in its capacity to export more than it imports did not govern trade with the colonies, where exchange was not equal and the surplus imported reflected the prevalence of unpaid-for monopoly gains rather than the output of precious metals.

> The general interest of Spain in such trade [with America], like that of all nations with colonies consists in transferring many products and merchandise from Europe and bringing back there much from the Americas. Any economic arrangement under this trade which does not lead to this end will only have disastrous foundations and must be spurned. The general maxim of trade, which demands that a state transfer much and bring little in, does not hold for trade with America. The nations which have colonies

there will never obtain many products for the amount of wealth transferred from Europe: and the more is brought in in products, merchandise, the more is transferred and the easier abundant transfers become.

They also understood that this trade helped consolidate one of the most salient aspects of dependence: the existence of a class whose way of life and wealth can neither be met nor satisfied by local production.

The luxury among residents [of the colonies] brought about by trade, the opportunity it constantly offers them of procuring all life's comforts with the product of their own land, is the only motive urging them to work and to make the colonies increasingly richer productionwise.

Commerce, Colonialism, and Corruption in Central America

ROBERT W. PATCH

Robert W. Patch, in *Maya and Spaniard in Yucatán, 1648–1812* (1993), argues that "Yucatán was not an isolated province, for it possessed resources that were exploited and used to effect integration into the world economy. . . . " (p. 4). This view contrasts sharply with the position taken by Nany Farriss in her magisterial *Maya Society Under Colonial Rule: The Collective Enterprise of Survival* (1984), which emphasizes "Yucatán's 'commercial isolation' and lack of export opportunities" (p. 36).

The selection on colonial Central America reprinted here extends Patch's interest in trade, commerce, indigenous society, and the formation of markets. Like Enrique Semo's contribution, Patch's view of the impact of international trade on colonial Latin America is difficult to categorize in orthodox dependency or world-system terms. Patch argues that the integration of Central America (called Guatemala under the Spaniards, but it included

Robert Patch, "Imperial Politics and Local Economy in Colonial Central America, 1670–1770," *Past & Present* (May 1994), pp. 77–80, 101–107.

Mexican Chiapas and modern El Salvador, Honduras, Nicaragua, and Costa Rica) into the larger international economy did not destroy the indigenous cotton industry. Just the opposite occurred. The industry expanded because Spanish royal officials sought to profit from it. The Spaniards organized a kind of compulsory putting-out system (the *repartimiento*) in which cotton grown in the lowlands was sent up to the highland provinces to be woven. Some of the cloth was sent to Mexico, but most was consumed in the silver and indigo-producing regions of Tegucigalpa (Honduras) and San Salvador. Patch views the *repartimiento* as a means of integrating the trading network of Central America and of providing inputs to industries that linked Central America to Mexico, Peru, and Europe. Moreover, Patch emphasizes the impact that existing indigenous structures of production had on the shaping of Spanish colonialism. There was, as Patch sometimes puts it, considerable local autonomy within the construction of an export economy.

Although the Maya people of Guatemala were clearly exploited by the *repartimiento*, Patch concludes that it helped ensure their survival as well. Patch was a student of Stanley Stein at Princeton, and his intellectual debt to Stein is clear. In an influential essay published in 1973 in the book *Research in Mexican History*, Stein observed that the kind of economic system that Patch found in colonial Guatemala addressed the inadequacies of a purely market mechanism. Patch confirms this observation, for it was the Spanish officials' use of political power to create local monopolies that allowed them to extract profits from Indian communities by purchasing materials cheaply and inflating the prices of finished goods.

Colonialism was very good business for Spaniards and Portuguese in America. By the middle of the seventeenth century the revenues pouring in to the Portuguese treasury from the sugar exports of Brazil were so enormous that King John IV could baldly refer to the South American colony as his "milch cow". What was true for Portugal was even more true for Spain: 16,887 tons of silver and 1,813 tons of gold from America were registered in Spanish ports between 1501 and 1650, and probably even more was smuggled in at the same time. Still larger quantities were dispatched to Spain during the next century and a half. These remittances of precious metals from America allowed the Spanish kings to maintain their power in Europe when their European resources alone would have been insufficient for that task. Perhaps even more importantly, commercial profits earned by private individuals in both the Portuguese and Spanish empires greatly surpassed the share acquired by the Iberian monarchs. Colonialism, in short, led to both commercial expansion and increased government revenues for Portugal and Spain.

To maximize their shares of the benefits of colonialism, the Iberian governments had to minimize their expenditures in America. The Spanish crown, unlike the Portuguese, could accomplish this to a great extent by relying on native political élites to enforce colonial rule. The result was that only a handful of royal officials was sufficient to rule over millions of Indians; "Spain governs, but does not administer", in the words of Pierre Chaunu. Minimizing administrative costs also meant keeping the bureaucracy small and salaries low.

Needless to say, these penny-pinching policies had their own costs. This essay seeks to explain how the Spanish government held down administrative expenses in the kingdom of Guatemala (a political entity embracing what are now the Central American republics of Guatemala, El Salvador, Honduras, Nicaragua and Costa Rica, as well as the Mexican state of Chiapas). It will also analyse the costs resulting from that policy. One of these is what, in modern parlance, is called governmental corruption.

The ultimate result, however, was much more than simply corruption. An entire commercial system based on government officials came into existence. The Spanish *corregidores* (magistrates), *alcaldes mayores* (high magistrates) and governors who ruled in the kingdom of Guatemala in reality were entrepreneurs who organized a variety of business activities that effected the economic integration of the whole of Central America. They succeeded because their political power allowed them to use coercion, rather than market forces, to get the local population, especially the Indian peasantry, to comply with their demands. Colonialism was thus an essential feature of commercial exchange, for market forces alone would not have resulted in the transfer of profits away from the peasants on the scale desired by the merchant class. Political power allowed magistrates in Central America to isolate the producers from merchant competitors and acquire the lion's share of the surplus.

At the same time, professional merchants, rather than competing with the government official, became their partners in crime — for the activities were of course illegal — and funnelled capital to the magistrates who used their political power to make the investments yield a profit. This was accomplished by ensuring the enforcement of contracts and collection of debts—which economic power alone could not always accomplish. Moreover political power could be used to establish local monopolies, thereby eliminating troublesome competitors. In fact, in other contexts, the need to acquire political power to enforce commercial contracts and exclude foreign commercial interlopers was one of the major causes of European colonial expansion.

In Spanish Central America, then, the servants of the state served as essential intermediaries between European capital and American peasants and landowners. Government officials helped mobilize and invest capital, channelled the surplus away from producers, and then split the profits with their merchant partners. In short, the state played a leading role in capital accumulation under colonialism. "Corruption" was therefore an integral and necessary part of the colonial system. It was the means of maintaining a bureaucracy at little cost, and considerable benefit, to the crown. It provided the government with people who volunteered their services to the state in return for the opportunity to enrich themselves. Commercial opportunities, however, were limited by the availability of human as well as natural resources. Imperial political structure was thus intimately related to the local economy and society. Colonialism in Central America benefited the Spaniards because imperial demands interacted with, and adapted to, the local ecology, people and structures of production. . . .

By the middle of the eighteenth century the business enterprises of the magistrates were known collectively as the *repartimiento*. Except for the twenty years between 1759 and 1779, these activities were illegal. Nevertheless the crown tolerated the enterprises of its officials as long as the Indians were not provoked into outright rebellion. As a result, for over a century magistrates were routinely charged with violating the law and then not only pardoned for the offence but even commended for their actions. Only a handful whose greed surpassed accepted bounds was removed from office or subjected to serious fines.

The *repartimiento* system, however, cannot be understood merely as a form of tolerated corruption. It was much more than that. It was above all else a commercial system integrating the provinces of the kingdom of Guatemala. It tied regions of different ecological conditions into a network of trade based on regional specialization and division of labour. Cotton was produced in the valleys and coastal lowlands, especially in Verapaz and in the Nicaraguan magistracies, and transported to highland Guatemala and Chiapa to be made into thread and textiles. The goods manufactured in Chiapa, however, did not stay there, for they had a long way to go before reaching their markets. The textiles, as well as the cochineal and cacao acquired through other *repartimientos*, were sent north, by mule, to Oaxaca in New Spain. However, taking cotton textiles and cochineal to Oaxaca resembled carrying coals to Newcastle, for Oaxaca was itself a major producer and exporter of those same goods. Chiapa's real trade was with Mexico. The Province's skirts (*chiapanecas*) were even imitated in New Spain. Some cochineal from Chiapa was exported to Spain.

Textiles from highland Guatemala may also have gone north to Mexico. Most, however, were sent to the mining camps of Tegucigalpa (highland Honduras), to the cities and villages of the indigo-producing province of San Salvador, and to the capital of Santiago, where the large-scale merchant houses handled the magistrates' goods and arranged for the investment of the capital that made the wheels of trade turn. Silver and indigo — produced in part as a result of the capital invested by magistrates and their merchant partners — in turn were exported to Peru, Mexico and Europe. Cacao was also produced, sold locally and exported to Spain and New Spain.

The kingdom of Guatemala was thus characterized by regional specialization. The highlands of Chiapa and Guatemala produced the textiles needed in the silver- and indigo-producing regions of Tegucigalpa and San Salvador. The latter two provinces were two more links of the commercial chain tying magistrates from several provinces together into a network of trading relationships and vested interest. Tegucigalpa, San Salvador and, to a lesser extent, Sonsonate produced the vital raw materials exported beyond Central America to Peru, Mexico and Europe. In turn, Tegucigalpa and San Salvador served as the importers of the manufactured goods and foodstuffs produced in the other provinces. Much of the cotton textile manufacturing carried out in the highland Guatemalan provinces of overwhelmingly Maya population was a backward linkage of the export economies of the largely mestizo and mulatto provinces of modern-day El Salvador and Honduras.

Even Nicaragua was an important component of the interregional trading network of Central America. The Nicaraguan magistracies exported nothing to Europe, a little indigo and dye-wood to Peru and a substantial quantity of raw cotton to the textile-manufacturing centres of the kingdom. Some of this reached Chiapa, which exported textiles to Mexico but had to import raw materials for its industry. Thus Nicaraguan cotton, once spun and woven, probably ended up as far north as New Spain.

A large part of this commercial activity was carried out, organized or even monopolized by government officials. Their business activities, especially in cotton textiles, were the Spanish American equivalent of the famous South and East Asian "country trade" that Europeans engaged in, dealing in goods demanded in Asia in order to acquire the goods demanded in Europe. The Spanish officials traded in a variety of items sold throughout America in order to get exports for Spain. It was to a great extent due to the magistrates that Central America was tied, directly or indirectly, into the world economy. *Corregidores, alcaldes mayores* and governors, in short, played vital entrepreneurial roles by helping integrate the provinces into the kingdom and the kingdom into the empire.

At the same time the *repartimiento*'s involvement with the Indians became one of the most important mechanisms for extracting a surplus from the Indians. Tribute, once the most important mechanism for channelling wealth away from the peasantry to support the colonial élites, eventually became simply an adjunct to the magistrates' business. It is important to note that *repartimientos* of money or credit were usually carried out on St John's Day (24 June) and at Christmas; by no small coincidence, those dates happened to be when tribute payments were due. By the middle of the eighteenth century many Indians no longer paid their goods and money directly to their caciques, who then delivered them to the magistrates, as in the past; rather, governors, *alcaldes mayores* and *corregidores* had their business partners in Santiago pay the tribute to the exchequer. The payment was treated as a normal business expense of the commercial companies which magistrates established with important merchants of the capital. Tribute in effect was the king's share of the profits. The *repartimiento*, by absorbing the tributary system, became the most important mechanism for extracting wealth from the peasants and for incorporating the Indians of Central America into the regional and world economies.

The commercial system run by the magistrates worked so well

because it took advantage of an already existing sexual division of labour. Forced labour systems, after all, are not limited to the heavy tasks — usually carried out by males — of digging, hauling, planting or harvesting. In the well-developed peasant economy of Central America, agriculture was the exclusive domain of Indian males, who produced not only the maize but also the wheat, cacao, wool and cotton, that is, the raw materials so important as trade goods. Quantitatively the most valuable goods of all, however, were textiles and thread, the products of the female sector of the domestic economy. The *repartimiento* in Central America was thus the means by which local government officials tapped the surplus labour of men, women and children: that is, the entire peasant community.

The *repartimiento* also worked well because it took advantage of already existing structures of production. Spinning, weaving and cultivation of cotton and cacao were traditional branches of the Indian economy; in most places new productive processes were not needed. True, silver-mining and large-scale indigo-production were new, having been introduced by the Spaniards, but these activities only affected the native people of Tegucigalpa, Chiquimula and San Salvador. Disruption of the Indians was thus limited to a few places. For the most part, especially in the highlands of Chiapa and Guatemala, the native people were left alone — as long as they produced the goods desired by the Spaniards. Economic exploitation and commercialization, while disruptive in some contexts, were perfectly compatible with Indian traditions, and thus native culture had a better chance of adapting to colonialism rather than succumbing to the excessive demands of the colonists. To this day, the Guatemalan and Chiapan highlands — the textile manufacturing regions containing the most lucrative magistracies in the kingdom — are among the most Indian parts of Latin America.

Integration into the world economy therefore did not necessarily result in societal destruction. What counted was the nature of that integration. The modern world-system may often have forced non-European peoples into slavery or "coerced cash crop" production — to borrow a well-known phrase from Wallerstein — but at other times the international economy demanded not the elimination but the perpetuation or even expansion of native industry. This provided the economic base for a people's survival. In the kingdom of Guatemala the Maya survived by continuing to manufacture cotton textiles. Although they were subjected to coercive economic relationships resulting from colonialism, they became neither slaves nor serfs in the world-system. Moreover their production made Central America into an export platform which, like India and China, sent its textiles not to the core European economy but rather to other regional economies of Spanish America. Manufacturing, far from disappearing in the Europe-dominated world economy, remained an essential element of local, non-western structures of production. To be sure, it did not serve as a "proto-industrialization" stage preparatory to modern industrial capitalism. Nevertheless it was an important, and even expanding, economic sector of the non-European world long after contact with or conquest by Europeans.

Despite the commercial viability and profitability of the *repartimiento*, the Spanish government never reconciled itself to the participation of its officials in large-scale commercial activities. The system, after all, was coercive: the Indians were forced to participate. Considerable abuses naturally resulted, and in fact on several occasions revolts occurred because of the excesses perpetrated by the magistrates. Moreover the collaboration of the native élite, who enforced the magistrates' will in the villages, eventually led many Indians to question the legitimacy of their own rulers. The *repartimiento* eventually undermined the authority of the native ruling class, and at times led to rebellions not only against the Spaniards but also against the Indian village leaders.

The crown also objected to the economic results of the *repartimiento* system. The royal magistrates made their enterprises profitable by using their political power to prevent competing merchants from conducting business in the provinces under their jurisdiction. The system thus in effect led to the establishment of local monopolies and concomitant economic abuses. Inevitably the magistrates represented themselves and their merchant partners better than they represented the interests of the king. As a Visitor-General to another part of America succinctly explained the problem, "It is not easy, or even possible, to improve the local government of the provinces . . . as long as its chief officials or *corregidores* are businessmen".

These views were to be the basis of, and justification for, the Bourbon reform programme and bureaucratic expansion of the last decades of the eighteenth century. In effect Spain was undergoing the same change in values that had already taken place in England: those who dispensed justice were now expected to be unbiased and honest. Officials in Spain had finally come to understand the business activities of magistrates in America in modern terms: that is, as a manifestation of governmental corruption.

The Wages of Imperialism: Europe

PATRICK O'BRIEN

Patrick O'Brien is the author (with Caglar Keyder) of *Economic Growth in Britain and France, 1780–1914: Two Paths to the Twentieth Century* (1978), *The Economic Effects of the American Civil War* (1988), and a number of other books and papers. O'Brien's argument, like Stanley Lebergott's which follows, is that European trade with the peripheral economies in Latin America, the Caribbean, the southern colonies of British North America, Africa, and Asia formed only a small proportion of all European trade in the early modern period. Moreover, trade itself was but a small part of Europe's overall economic activity. Even if this trade was very profitable, O'Brien argues, it could not have accounted for much of Europe's investment in this period. Since investment is the source of economic growth, O'Brien is basically arguing that Europe's trade with the periphery could not have been an important source of European capital accumulation, and hence of European growth. But this runs counter to the spirit of much dependency and world-system analysis, which emphasizes just the opposite.

Looking at the composition of European imports from the peripheral economies, O'Brien saw no reason to alter his conclusions. Reductions in the import of sugar, coffee, tea, tobacco, and cotton might have had significant short-run effects on production, but in the long run, O'Brien argues, substitution of sources of supply and changes in the character of productive activity would have taken place. Nor did importing specie from the New World change the picture much, for as O'Brien puts it, silver from the mines of Mexico and Peru acted as a lubricant to production and not as energy itself. He seems to emphasize the effects of silver

Patrick O'Brien, "European Economic Development: The Contribution of the Periphery," *The Economic History Review*, Second Series, 35:1 (1982), pp. 1–3, 7–8, 9–14, 17. Reprinted by permission of The Economic History Review.

output on the European price level, rather than on European production properly speaking. Even the notion of a world economy in this period is suspect, according to O'Brien, because of frequent and unpredictable interruptions in international trade.

O'Brien's position, then, is that there is little empirical support for one aspect of both dependency and world-systems thinking. Yet there may still be merit in a view that emphasizes innovation in the organization and conduct of trade in this period as an important adjunct of European growth. Recent studies of the Atlantic slave trade and its development emphasize, as Franklin Knight put it (in a 1991 volume edited by Barbara Solow entitled *Slavery and the Rise of the Atlantic System*), that slavery and the slave trade contributed to the development of market economies in the Portuguese and Spanish empires. For example, the far-flung slave trade created an international marketing mechanism that made faster economic growth in the Atlantic economy possible. One should bear this point in mind in reading O'Brien's important essay.

Economic history has enjoyed a revival in the study of development. Provocative interpretations of the course and causes of long-term growth continue to emerge from the writings of Immanuel Wallerstein, Gunder Frank and Samir Amin. While the basic purpose of their research is to explore the origins of underdevelopment, their commitment to a "global perspective" has led them into wide ranging excursions into the economic history of Western Europe because, to quote Wallerstein, "Neither the development nor underdevelopment of any specific territorial unit can be analyzed or interpreted without fitting it into the cyclical rhythms and secular trends of the world economy as a whole".

According to the new school of development history the critical period when different parts of the world set off along contrasting paths of economic growth occurred between 1450 and 1750—three centuries which witnessed the emergence and consolidation of "European world economy based upon the capitalist mode of production". The evolution of trade and commerce under this old international economic order (over long cycles of expansion (1450–1600), stagnation (1600–1750), and upswing again from the middle of the eighteenth century) created conditions for development and underdevelopment in the nineteenth and twentieth centuries. As they perceive it, the relative backwardness of Asia, Africa, Latin America,

and Eastern Europe, which became visible after 1800, originated in
the mercantile era when Western Europe turned the terms and conditions for international trade heavily in its favour. Through the deployment of military power and superior forms of state organization, the Europeans either plundered and colonized territories in
Asia, Africa, and the Americas or reduced weaker economies to
conditions of dependency. They actively promoted or encouraged
forms of labour control (slavery, peonage, serfdom) at the periphery
(sharecropping in the semi-periphery) which maintained the cost of
producing exports for Western Europe close to the level of subsistence wages. Patterns of trade evolved in which the mineral wealth
and primary products of the periphery were exchanged for the manufactured goods and high quality farm produce of the core on
highly unequal terms. Over time, such patterns of specialization
pushed the economies of Western Europe towards industrialization
and higher standards of living and the economies of the periphery
towards primary production, monoculture, and far lower levels of
per capita income.

Summaries are simplifications, and distortions occur in "box-
ing" scholars together in "schools". Obviously there are salient differences in the treatment and coverage of global history from one
author to another and in the precise significance imputed to the effects of international economic relations on long-term development.
Furthermore, the new school's primary concern is with the economic development of the periphery and the distribution of gains
from trade and not with the economic history of Western Europe.
But I do not propose to consider the view that specialization on primary produce for export to Europe, together with the modes of
labour control utilized by the economies of the periphery, hampered
their long term evolution towards industrial societies. Nor will I attempt to unravel the logical and empirical difficulties involved in the
application of the concept of unequal exchange to the history of
commerce between nations. For present purposes I can accept the
view that restraints on the evolution of free markets for labour and
impediments to the reallocation of resources from primary production to industry and urban services hindered progress towards a
modern economy. Any there can be no dispute that rewards from
participation in foreign trade were unequally distributed during the
mercantile era when military force formed an integral part of the international economic order. My response to the new history of de-

velopment will be rigidly confined to the views its authors have promulgated about the "significance" for Western Europe of its connexions with markets and sources of supply at the periphery. The hypotheses, which are of central importance for the economic history of Western Europe, can be abbreviated and tabulated as follows:

(a) the long-run growth of Western Europe in general, and Britain in particular, can only be meaningfully analyzed on a global scale;

(b) the expansion of the international economy for some three centuries after 1750 generated supernormal profits which became steadily more concentrated in the hands of the capitalists of certain core states;

(c) their investments made a "large" contribution to the accumulation of capital in Western Europe; and by the end of the eighteenth century this region had been placed on a path of economic growth which left other parts of the world (the periphery and the semi-periphery) in conditions of underdevelopment.

(d) furthermore, spinoffs and externalities from trade with the periphery (operating through specialization and the acquisition of key imports, particularly bullion) promoted the economic growth of Western Europe in decisive ways.

Clearly it is necessary for historians of Europe to analyze connexions between the mercantile era and the progress of industrialization after 1750. They have not neglected foreign trade and where relevant they will adopt a "global perspective". But I wish to argue that commerce between core and periphery for three centuries after 1450 proceeded on a small scale, was not a uniquely profitable field of enterprise, and while it generated some externalities, they could in no way be classified as decisive for the economic growth of Western Europe. In brief, the commerce between Western Europe and regions at the periphery of the international economy forms an insignificant part of the explanation for the accelerated rate of economic growth experienced by the core after 1750. I propose to conduct my argument within the geo-political categories, world systems perspectives, and time spans adumbrated by the new history of development. The debate has been set up in these terms and will surely continue at local, national, and continental levels. . . .

Since Britain traded with and invested in continents on a far larger scale than any other European country (with the possible exception of Holland), it appears that the conclusions offered by historians of world economic systems and accumulation on a world scale exaggerate the impact of inter-continental trade on capital formation in Western Europe in the early stages of industrialization. Their misplaced emphasis has arisen basically because they failed to consider the place of trade in relation to the totality of economic activity and also because they remain convinced that commerce with the periphery (based upon "exploitation", "unequal exchange", and "pillage") must have been a uniquely profitable field of enterprise. To support this view the new school has marshalled vivid descriptions of tropical trades, selective data on profits, and several graphic quotations from Adam Smith, Karl Marx, and Maynard Keynes. Despite the authority of that formidable trio, it is fair to observe that their assertions have not been supported by the evidence required to demonstrate that *average* rates of profit which European capitalists derived from investment and trade with Africa, Asia, and tropical America rose persistently above the rates of return which they could have earned on feasible investments, at home or indeed elsewhere in the world economy.

What stands out from the meagre range of statistics collated together by Dutch, French, and English historians is the considerable degree of variance from one trade to another and from one year to another. Tropical trades appear to have been risky and the lucrative rewards reaped in the favourable circumstances of one voyage could easily be transformed into losses on another. Recent attempts to measure returns come up with average rates of profit over the long run around or below the 10 per cent mark. Furthermore, the long-run decline in the prices of sugar, pepper, coffee, tobacco, and tea on the commodity markets of Amsterdam, London, and Paris over the second half of the seventeenth century does not suggest that abnormal profits were sustained in these trades. Whatever may have happened during the long sixteenth century, the vastly increased volume of tropical imports carried into European ports after 1650 forced down prices to fractions of their original levels when sugar and tropical products were the luxuries of the rich. Elastic supplies of fairly homogeneous commodities and competition of the kind conducted between Portuguese, English, Dutch, and French merchants is not normally congruent with the persistence of supernormal profits.

On the contrary, the standard conditions for the maintenance of monopoly profits in international trade appear to have been present only in a diluted form for the majority of trades operating between Europe and other continents over the mercantile era. To survey the economic organization of commerce conducted by European nations with Africa, Asia, and tropical America is beyond the scope of this paper. But if British commerce with its Atlantic and Caribbean colonies is a significant example for the hypothesis of monopoly profits then recent research on the effects of the Navigation Acts and the profitability of the West Indies demonstrates it to be unfounded. . . .

Connexions between trade and growth are not exhausted by a consideration of trade's impact on the accumulation of capital. And the new history of development is also properly concerned with the gains Western Europe derived from the patterns of specialization promoted by trade with other continents. As Wallerstein observed, "the inclusion of Eastern Europe and Hispanic America into European world economy in the sixteenth century not only provided capital (through booty and high profit margins) but also liberated some labour in the core areas for specialization in other tasks. The occupational range of tasks in the core areas was a very complex one. It included a large remnant parallel to those in the periphery (for example, grain production). But the trend in the core was towards variety and specialization while the trend in the periphery was towards monoculture". But as trade with the periphery formed a small share of total trade and a tiny percentage of gross product, unless that trade generated important externalities, its impact (on specialization, innovation, institutional change, and other factors promoting growth at the core) *would have been in proportion to its relationship to total economic activity.* But a closer examination of the imports from Asia and the Americas might bring out particular commodities which created new and significant possibilities for production. Although tables of exports and imports broken down into standard groups cannot be drawn up, Mauro's flow chart reveals that the pressures towards specialization derived from such imports would have been rather limited. It is difficult to see how the purchase of spices, sugar, tea, coffee, rice, tropical fruit, hardwoods, dyestuffs, gold, and silver led to large gains from the reallocation of labour and other resources which increased possibilities for production in core economies. Trade between the continents simply allowed Europeans to escape from a fixed endowment of natural resources and to consume a mix of exotic commodities which could not be grown or mined in Western Europe. These crops did not compete directly with domestic agriculture, except in so far as tea and coffee reduced demand for beer and other beverages made from grain. Gains from trade consisted basically of a preferred pattern of consumption—not for masses of Europeans who lived during the mercantile era, but for those groups who could afford to buy tropical produce. Demand for sugar, tea, and coffee proved to be both income- and price-elastic, and consumption of such "luxuries" spread slowly down the social scale. But long-run gains from specialization, the division of labour, and the forces of competition—all of which flow from international trade—originated overwhelmingly in exchanges between and within European countries and far less from trade with other continents. . . .

It is also relevant to consider the contribution to European industrialization of the import of "essential" raw materials, foodstuffs, and industrial commodities—which might have reduced constraints on long-run supply or exercised demonstration effects which led to the expansion of production. Long before the discovery of the Americas, Europeans had successfully transplanted rice, sugar, sorghum, cotton, citrus fruits, and silk worms into Italy, Iberia, and Southern France. From the Americas came a whole range of new crops including maize, potatoes, groundnuts, beans, tobacco, cocoa, pineapples, tomatoes, red peppers, and chillies, which added variety to the European diet. But their introduction into European agriculture contributed only marginally to the supplies of calories available before and during the Industrial Revolution. Pineapples, cocoa, and groundnuts grew in botanical gardens, and tobacco and tomatoes spread slowly. Only maize and potatoes raised the capacity of agriculture to support population growth. Maize eventually did increase grain supplies from Southern Europe but its real impact came after the mid-nineteenth century. And although the potato helped to stimulate population growth in Ireland, and to feed the working people of England, Belgium, and Germany, the new vegetable was never a critical element in food supplies in the eighteenth or indeed for most of the nineteenth century.

Sugar refining, tobacco processing, the final transformation of tea, coffee and cocoa into drinkable beverages and, above all, the manufacture of cotton textiles certainly began and prospered in Western Europe through trade with the periphery. The English cotton industry developed by imitating muslins, nankeens, and other "stuffs" imported by the East India company. It followed the classic pattern of import substitution where foreign (in this case Indian and Chinese) manufactured goods pioneered the market, and domestic substitutes gradually replaced imports—assisted, of course, by protection. Such industries, together with the employment and profits they generated, would have been inconceivable without an assured supply of raw materials from Asia and the Americas. Nevertheless the advantages of other continents in the cultivation of tobacco and sugar were not absolute. Both crops could be grown in Southern Europe, and tobacco cultivation in France and Britain had been restricted in the interests of the colonies. By the 1830s sugar beet had appeared in France and Germany as a viable substitute for cane sugar.

The crux of the matter is really to quantify the importance of industries which depended upon imported raw materials. Here statistics for Britain can again serve as outer-bound estimates for Western Europe as a whole. By 1841—a year well into the First Industrial Revolution—cotton textiles accounted for about 7 per cent of gross national product, and food-processing industries, utilizing raw materials imported from the periphery, added a further 1 per cent. Since Britain industrialized before the rest of Europe there is no reason to claim that if Western Europe had been forced to manage without imported sugar, coffee, tea, tobacco, and cotton, its industrial output could have fallen by a large percentage. A decline of not more than 3 or 4 per cent in the industrial output of the core would seem to be the likely *short-run* effect from a total cut-off of imports. Over time that impact could be mitigated by patterns of substitution for tropical foodstuffs and raw materials and by the redeployment of labour and other factors of production from cotton textiles, tobacco processing, beverages, and sugar refining into other types of manufacturing activity. While cotton was certainly among the first industries to be transformed by mechanization and the factory mode of organization, only a simplistic growth model with cotton as a leading sector and with British innovation as the engine of Western European growth could support an argument that the Lancashire cotton industry was vital for the industrialization of the core. That process proceeded on too broad a front to be checked by the defeat of an advanced column whose supply lines stretched across the oceans to Asia and the Americas.

American treasure has been singled out by the new history of development for special emphasis. "The production of these precious metals", claims Gunder Frank, "was the principal functional contribution of the New World regions to the expansion of trade in the world, the accumulation of capital in the European metropolis and the development of capitalism". Bullion undoubtedly had an impact which transcended the effects of other imports because silver and gold formed an integral part of Western Europe's money supply. And money mattered between 1450 and 1750 when the spread of the market and monetary transactions (both within and between states) accompanied economic progress achieved by the core. Thus, while the potential significance of bullion imports is not in doubt, their actual importance has not been estimated, and the new historians simply elucidate mechanisms through which imported silver and gold assisted economic growth. As they describe it, bullion from the Americas:

(a) relieved an actual or potential monetary constraint on exchange and production;

(b) facilitated the expansion of international trade between Western Europe on the one hand and Asia and the Baltic on the other;

(c) exercised an upward pressure on price levels in core economies which redistributed income between workers and capitalists and encouraged trade to respond to differential rates of inflation within and between countries.

To substantiate claims made for the all-pervasive effects of bullion imports requires, however, a more explicit specification of relevant connexions and a greater attempt to gauge the importance of money in the growth process than anything found in the new history of development. To begin with the obvious question: how much did the import of some 181 tons of gold and 16,000 tons of silver between 1500 and 1660 add to monetary stocks in Western Europe? Data for money supplies do not exist, but Braudel and Spooner reject the notion that "the American mines poured their precious metals into a deprived Europe and so precipitated a sudden change" because "the accumulated stocks in the Old World since early times represented a considerable monetary mass". They doubt "if the inflow of precious metals from the New World did not even reach one half—on the most optimistic hypothesis—of the old stock of European money . . . ". On their own estimate, as late as 1650 the inflow had added not more than 25 per cent to the existing stock of silver and gold in Europe.

Europe's own mines expanded production by a factor of five between 1460 and 1530 and had effectively relieved the "silver famine" of the late fifteenth century before any real quantity of American treasure arrived in Spain. In addition, paper or fictive money "invaded" the economic life of Europe during the mercantile era, but it remained a small but growing part of total circulation. Although core countries were, apparently, not ready for paper money, their rulers utilized debasement frequently enough to obtain the means to pay for their military and other expenditures. Provided debased currency exchanged for commodities at prices above the intrinsic value of the specie contained in the coins, this device added to the supply of cash for transactions within national territories. By the second half of the sixteenth century prospects for the circulation of debased coins closer to face value improved, when governments stipulated that royal coins would be accepted at par in payment for taxes. As the royal tax base spread into the economy this proclamation weakened the link between specie and money. Coins of the realm were on the way to becoming legal tender. Finally, the diffusion within Europe of credit instruments and the development of financial intermediaries increased the velocity of circulation—alas, by some unknown percentage. "Whether as coin or as bills of exchange money cascaded from person to person and from money market to money market."

Western Europe demanded more money for increased trade, the division of labour, population growth, urbanization, the shift from barter transactions, and the growth of public expenditure. But imported specie was only one of several means utilized within the region to cope with a potential monetary restraint on internal trade and production. Europe's own silver and copper provided some of the money. Merchants and financiers pushed up the velocity of circulation, and by debasement European rulers reduced the weight of specie required for each coin of account. There can be no presumption that the silver and gold of the Americas carried most of the monetary load required for economic expansion after 1500 or that Europeans would have found it excessively difficult and costly to develop either paper substitutes or a fiat coinage if silver from Mexico and Peru and gold from New Granada and Brazil had remained underground. Money was a lubricant not a source of power—oil but not petroleum. . . .

What this exercise in counterfactual history suggests is that *if* the British economy had been excluded from trade with the periphery, gross annual investment expenditures would have fallen by not more than 7 per cent. All biases in these calculations (which refer to decades after the onset of the Industrial Revolution) run in favour of the hypothesis that this commerce provided a large share of the reinvestible surplus; and Britain, to reiterate the point, traded with other continents on a far larger scale than other European countries.

There is, moreover, no evidence in the admittedly poor data now available that "average" rates of profit earned on capital in commerce with the periphery were "supernormal". Over wide areas of tropical trades competition between the merchants of several maritime powers operated to hold prices of commodities and the returns to capital below monopolistic levels. And the significance of the periphery cannot be inflated much beyond its share in national product by reference to externalities or to imports, described as decisive for the growth of the core. Trade in tropical produce gave rise to far greater opportunities for consumption than possibilities for production, and the view that American bullion was indispensable for economic progress in Western Europe is almost certainly untenable.

The Wages of Imperialism:
The United States

STANLEY LEBERGOTT

Stanley Lebergott has written several important books—*Manpower in Economic Growth: The American Record Since 1800* (1966), *The American Economy: Income, Wealth, and Want* (1976), and *Pursuing Happiness: American Consumers in the Twentieth Century* (1993)—as well as a number of other influential studies. The article reproduced here, although not as well known, is a very useful complement to Patrick O'Brien's essay.

Stanley Lebergott, "The Returns to U.S. Imperialism, 1890–1929," *The Journal of Economic History*, 40: 2 (1980), pp. 229–237, 241–242, 249. Reprinted with the permission of Cambridge University Press.

Some of Lebergott's arguments are similar to O'Brien's. He finds, for example, that the share of foreign investment in total United States investment between 1869 and 1929 was very small, and that the role of profits from foreign investment in the domestic economy was correspondingly minor. Moreover, the impact of United States investments on the recipient economies was, in Lebergott's view, rather more beneficial than its critics generally assume. In Cuba, for instance, Lebergott argues that commercial agreements between the United States and Cuba gave Cubans a preferred position in the United States sugar market and so drove up the value of Cuban land. Real wages in Cuba rose as well, because the demand for labor increased. In Panama, Lebergott finds military gains and gains to ocean shippers in general, but few purely economic gains that were of benefit only to United States interests. Finally, the inflow of capital investment from the United States eroded the monopoly position of entrepreneurs in the host countries, thereby driving down monopoly profits. Lebergott's provocative conclusion is worth quoting: "The heart of the anti-imperialist struggle, then, may prove to be a squabble between two capitalist groups, one native and the other foreign, fighting over the spoils of progress."

Imperialism is a moderately ingenious system in which residents of capitalist nations are forced to transfer income among themselves. The transfer mechanism creates extraterritorial impacts as well. It increases workers' incomes in colonial nations. It benefits their landowners. And it strikes down their business monopolies. (That these benefits are conferred on developing nations helps distinguish imperialism from other modes of subsidy to business such as tariff protection.) This process creates an aura of generous patronage in the imperializing power. It stimulates a sense of outrage in the colonial nation. And it speeds the advancement of military leaders in both. Such lively consequences have obscured the primary economic struggle under imperialism—which is not between capitalists from the imperium and oppressed peasants, but between different groups of capitalists. . . .

Between the Civil War and 1897 American foreign investment rose from a mere $75 million to $685 million; it then rose by nearly $20 billion from 1897 to 1929. "Under the old capitalism," Lenin wrote, "the export of goods was a most typical feature. Under modern capitalism, when monopolies prevail, the export of capital has become the typical feature." Rosa Luxemburg declared, "Imperialism is the political expression of the accumulation of capital in its competitive struggle for what remains still open of the non-capitalist environment."

The increases in U.S. foreign investment were indeed impressive. But most numbers for continental economies look big, whether for the United States or China. How do they look when dimensioned against the entire flow of U.S. investment? Of all U.S. investment from 1869 to 1897, the foreign share accounted for 1 percent; and from 1900 to 1929, the heyday of marine intervention, it accounted for only 6 percent. Put another way: From 1900 to 1929 the entire increase of U.S. foreign investment all over the globe did not equal the increased investment in California alone.

Did so small a foreign commitment really offer a vent for surplus capital? Was it indeed the *unum porro necessarium* that enabled U.S. capitalism to create its twentieth-century hegemony?

Any approach as comprehensive as Marxism-Leninism deals comprehensively with capitalism. It does not offer a theory of Macy's profitability, or Gimbel's, or even United Fruit's. It deals with the complex, contradictory vastness of capitalism. That theory implies that U.S. investment abroad during 1890–1929 was critical in propping up the overall profit rate on U.S. capital. If so, it should have affected that rate significantly. But U.S. overseas investments from 1890 to 1929 pushed the rate of return on U.S. capital from a bit over 4.8 percent to a bit under 4.9 percent. Did so tiny an increase stave off the inevitable collapse of capitalism? Or change its character?

Most U.S. industries didn't bother to invest abroad. The aggregate impact on the profitability of the U.S. investment was small. What did occur was the seizure of lush investment opportunities in a handful of sectors. Which industries were involved? Cleona Lewis's data on U.S. investments abroad offer us a guide. Her rich detail indicates that U.S. firms made substantial investments abroad in several industry categories. For only three of these—agriculture, manufacturing, and metals—was the ratio of foreign-to-U.S. investment more than a tenth of 1 percent. (Nor did ratios of foreign-to-domestic investment even reach 2 percent for these categories.)

For five industry/product groups, an important (significant?) ratio of foreign-to-U.S. investment appears.

1. Bananas: There were no domestic sources. Latin America provided the entire supply.
2. Sugar: All foreign sources provided about one fourth in 1897 and three fourths by 1929.
3. Copper: The share of foreign to total U.S. copper mine investment rose to perhaps 20 percent around 1900 and continued to be very substantial.
4. Oil: The foreign share rose from 3 percent in 1897 to 7 percent in 1929.
5. Precious metals: Foreign sources accounted for under 5 percent of U.S. investment.

Is there a common denominator to these concentrations of increase in U.S. foreign investment? Precious metal investment, indulged in by states from ancient Greece and the Inca empire to Soviet Russia, hardly requires any view on the theory of imperialism. The major categories—bananas, sugar, copper and oil—however, may be linked to market opportunities involving the trusts that developed in the period 1889–1900.

For bananas and sugar, U.S. trusts integrated vertically. They thereby protected themselves against combinations at the production level that might skim off their monopoly profits. By investing in banana plantations United Fruit assured its supply, and prevented any combination against it at either the farm or transport level. The American Sugar Refining Company actually had been confronted by a developing alliance of American sugar producers. U.S. beet sugar producers had expanded their output under the happy influence of the McKinley tariff. They then joined with the Louisiana cane sugar producers to block the Cuban Reciprocity Treaty. If successful they could then have raised tariffs against both Hawaiian and foreign sugar, thereby forcing the trust to divide its monopoly profits with a patriotic domestic cartel. By helping to keep the reciprocity door open, then, the trust guaranteed its supply of sugar and at the cost of only a minimum investment in Cuba by the trust itself.

Amalgamated's 30 percent stock price increase from 1898 to 1899–1901 had notified many investors of the potentially vast profits in copper. That point was italicized by the jump in its market yield (from about 2 percent in 1899 to 8 percent in the next two years). Moreover, dividends of the Michigan companies in 1899–1901 ran almost 50 percent above their 1898 level. Such prospects led both Morgan and the Guggenheims to invest heavily south of the border. They also induced other ardent investors— among them, Hearst, Frick, Haggin, and Ryan—to develop overseas copper mines. (Perhaps a more prudent trust might not have ignored the Secretan fiasco.)

It would require a more comprehensive review to determine how largely the actions of the new trusts were responsible for foreign investment in the turn-of-the-century years. For present purposes it may suffice to indicate that overseas investments by Americans in the period 1900 to 1929 do not seem particularly explicable by any general surplus of funds seeking overseas outlets. What characterized U.S. foreign investment over these decades was, instead, the seizing of the local opportunities here and there as avid entrepreneurs saw profit potential. These were pursued with no less zest than opportunities that appeared in North Dakota or New Mexico. In addition, attention concentrated on a few sectors (bananas, sugar and copper) where U.S. monopolies tried to protect future profit flows, or other entrepreneurs attempted to menace them.

Cuba

In April 1901 the occupying forces of the United States established a $1,000 prize to be known as "The Department of Agriculture stakes for Cuban bred horses and mares." General Wood, the American proconsul, was "acceding to the request of the 'Cuba Jockey Club' . . . [for] prizes at the horse races to be held at Buenavista, Havana course." And he expressed his fond hope "that the stakes will always be considered as the 'blue ribbon' of the Cuban turf."

This improbable but thoughtful gesture symbolized how varied were opportunities seized by special interests as they utilized the power and finance of the military government for their benefit. But what major U.S. economic interests benefited?

We take as our point of departure the example given in Lenin's succinct summary:

> Finance capital, concentrated in a few hands and exercising a virtual monopoly, exacts enormous and ever-increasing profits from the floating of companies, issues of stock, state loans, etc., tightens the grip of financial oligarchies and levies tribute upon the whole of society for the benefit of monopolists. Here is one example, taken from a multitude of others, of the methods of 'business' of the American trusts . . . the Sugar Trust set up monopoly prices on

the market, which secured it such profits that it could pay 10 percent dividend on capital "watered" sevenfold.

Imperialism centrally involved foreign investment. Mere market possibilities were perhaps primary in earlier stages of capitalism, but, Lenin states, had taken a secondary position under imperialism. Indeed a later review, by the major anti-imperialist historian of "our Cuban colony," noted that American exports to Cuba actually had fallen after the Spanish American War "as compared with those of Great Britain, France and Germany. . . . Our occupation had not promoted Cuba as a market for goods. . . . It is a common notion that people with specific economic interests beset legislators and governments with pressure to do things that will make them money. No doubt many of them do. Others need to be aroused to the work by those governments. American manufacturers in many states in 1902 and 1903 were far from anxious about export markets, or about a privileged position." But pressure by Roosevelt and unspecified "industry" finally brought the Congress to pass the Reciprocity Treaty. Of all the economic interest groups to be advantaged by this legislation, confirming the returns from the Cuban invasion, presumably the trust singled out by Lenin stood foremost.

Now what did the war and the Reciprocity Treaty do to the Sugar Trust and its profits? Did they increase the demand for sugar, thereby benefiting the trust? In 1899 U.S. consumers poured $190 million worth of sugar into their coffee, tea, and lemonade and bought a further $27 million to sweeten confectionery and soft drinks. The war, therefore, had not created the consumer's sweet tooth. Could it have shifted the demand curve for sugar in any significant fashion? There is no reason to think that it intensified the demand for Moxie. Nor did it increase the demand for other sugar products.

Did the war strengthen trust control of the U.S. market? As a tough enterprise the trust was already screwing as much out of the consumer as it could, war or no war. Its powers as a trust did not depend on either the Cubans or the war.

Gains to the Sugar Trust, therefore, must have been not on the demand but on the supply side. Jenks has written:

> On the face of the matter, the Reciprocity Treaty made a gift of .337 cents a pound on Cuban sugar to somebody from the United States Treasury. . . . (By 1910 . . . this benefit amounted to a total of twenty million dollars.) No one seems then to have known ex-

actly . . . where the .337 cents went. Most of it has gone . . . either to the ultimate consumers in the United States, or to the Atlantic refiners.

But Jenks's list includes those who did *not* benefit from the Reciprocity Treaty more surely than those who did.

Neither the war nor the treaty changed the supply of sugar. The Dutch were still producing in the East Indies. French, German, and American beet sugar producers were still producing. And the Hawaiians and Cubans were still producing. What the treaty did was award the Cubans a preferred market position. It cut the tariff margin between the price at which the Cubans sold and the price the American buyer had to pay.

If the American Sugar Refining Company had been the sole American purchaser of Cuban sugars it could have seized most, or all, of the reciprocity reduction. In fact, eight independent refining firms (some located on the west coast) bought over one third of U.S. raw sugar. Moreover, transport and refining costs were not changed by any of this. Hence, the benefit should have accrued almost wholly to Cuban producers. American taxpayers had simply begun to make an annual gift to Cuban sugar producers.

This is precisely and explicitly what was intended. In the authoritative words of Elihu Root, that gift permitted Cubans "to live," for the war's destruction had largely cut Cuban sugar production, and thereby Cuban incomes. Root declared:

> The peace of Cuba is necessary to the peace of the United States; the independence of Cuba is necessary to the safety of the United States. . . . The same considerations which led to the war with Spain now require that a commercial agreement be made under which Cuba can live.

The impact was immediate. Between 1900 and 1903 Cuban exports to the United States tripled, rising by 1.7 billion pounds. Concurrently, U.S. imports of Dutch East Indies sugar fell by 0.3 billion pounds, and imports of European (beet) sugar fell by 0.6 billion.

The Treaty, finest flower of American intervention in Cuba, had benefited neither the American consumer nor the Sugar Trust. It raised the gross receipts of Cuban sugar producers. These in turn had to pay increased rents to owners of Cuban land. For the price of the land had immediately risen, capitalizing the value of the delightful new tariff advantage. Hence the true beneficiaries were the owners of Cuban resources. As one Cuban planter told Congress, since the average developed field yielded $2\frac{1}{2}$ tons of sugar, "if you took off the duty" (of about $34 a ton) you would give a bounty of about $75 to "every acre of available sugar land in Cuba." The continuing gift from the American taxpayer, therefore, increased the value of Cuban land. That capital gain was unquestionably skimmed off by landowners in subsequent years whenever they sold or rented their land.

Who owned the land in 1899, just before the war, and thereby became prime beneficiaries of the treaty? Not the Trust. Indeed all Americans taken together controlled only 16 percent of the Cuban sugar crop as late as 1902.

The benefits of that advance could, of course, have been skimmed off if buyers had foreseen the passage of the treaty and had snapped up the land in advance. However, the Cuban mortgage law was changed in 1899 to prevent forced transfers of land in those turbulent times. And it kept the land in the hands of its pre-invasion owners. The land in 1902 remained "very largely in the hands of the people who had it on the 1st of January, 1899." It was, therefore, primarily the landowners as of 1899 who reaped the benefit of the revolution, invasion, and Reciprocity Treaty. And it was the owners of Cuban land not already in sugar who reaped the further benefits of continuing reciprocity as the sale of Cuban sugar in American markets expanded and expanded.

The prime economic beneficiaries of the Spanish-American War, in sum, were the Spaniards and Cubans who owned Cuban sugar land at the start of the war. The generous donor of benefits to these gentlemen turned out to be—the American taxpayer. For the latter's taxes had to make up for U.S. tariff revenue foregone by the Reciprocity Treaty. . . .

What of labor in Cuba? How did the American occupation and the Reciprocity Treaty affect Cuban labor? From 1900 to 1903 Cuban cane exports responded to the Treaty by tripling. Now tripling employment with little change in the population could only tend to drive up wages.

The obvious way for new American interests to nullify such pressures would have been to import low-cost contract labor from China. The Americans had done so in Hawaii. The Spaniards had once done so in Cuba. As Machado noted, however, Chinese labor "had been absolutely prohibited" for many years. Moreover, "public sentiment in Cuba would protest against introducing an inferior race, if any attempts were made to abolish the existing law." Did the U.S. military nonetheless impose such action at the behest of new American investors? On the contrary. Both Congress and the Executive sought to make Cuba the home of "the independent farmer and citizen," not of "the coolie": contract labor (largely Chinese) was therefore to be forbidden. In May 1902 the military governor dutifully forbade the importation of contract labor. Moreover, when the Reciprocity Treaty was finally passed it required Cuba to enact "immigration laws as rigorous as those of the United States."

Given an expanding U.S. market for Cuban sugar, together with a law forbidding the import of cheap labor, an excess demand for Cuban labor was inevitable. Hence Cuban wage rates tended to rise. Apparently they did rise. In 1900–1901, the average daily farm wage in the major sugar province of Mantanzas was 76¢. By January 1902, according to Colonel Bliss, the island average for common labor was $85^1/_2$¢ a day, a rise of over 10 percent. The "most inhuman oppression" should have led wage rates, and real income, to decline. The sequence of regulations, treaties, and investment by the American conquerors did not, however, yield such a decline. . . .

In summary, American imperialism after the Spanish American War worked systematic effects on economic interest groups in Latin America. (a) It increased the income of workers and peasants because it expanded the demand for labor. Moreover, anti-imperialist writers assure us that American companies in that expanding market paid wages that were average, and sometimes above average. (b) Workers' real wages often increased more than their money wages. The introduction of company stores ended monopolies once exercised by local general stores and taverns, thereby reducing the monopoly profits once provided by workers and peasants. (c) Imperialist investment increased the value of land held by local landholders, whether they held small plots of land or vast acreage. Such increases proved most substantial when the United States offered new and especially advantageous terms for native products entering the U.S. market (for example, as in Cuba). They also occurred whenever American companies bought land for plantations and railroads. The assertions by anti-imperialist writers that the United Fruit Company sometimes bought land through intermediaries suggest that American companies generally paid at least the price for land that native buyers did (and whenever the identity of the company became known, the company presumably paid somewhat above market prices). (d) American imperialism injured the vested interests of the existing native business group by destroying monopoly profits. The provision of general stores by American companies brought new competition to isolated farm and village areas. Such expansion inevitably menaced the monopoly profits of existing native entrepreneurs, even as it induced the creation of a new entrepreneurial group. Moreover, American investments would have snatched away opportunities that would-be native entrepreneurs saw, coveted, and sometimes might even have been able to finance. The heart of the anti-imperialist struggle, then, may prove to be a squabble between two capitalist groups, one native and the other foreign, fighting over the spoils of progress.

PART II

The Great Delay, 1820–1870

Independence brought few immediate benefits to the economies of Latin America. Inexpensive British cottons, for instance, could now find a larger market than they had under the Spaniards, but the collapse of silver mining during the wars of independence made paying for imports difficult. The mines of Guanajuato and Potosí had flooded, and their labor forces had been dispersed. The price of mercury, used in separating silver from its ore, rose sharply during the early 1830s and remained high for much of the century. And fewer specialized silver financiers (*rescatadores*) were to be found after independence. So silver production fell. Since silver was an important part of the colonial money supply, private lending also plummeted. At the same time, the flight of capital aggravated the contraction of credit. For instance, a group of twelve to fifteen wealthy Spaniards, reportedly bearing £2–£3 million ($10–$15 million), fled Mexico after a decree of expulsion in 1828. They settled in Bordeaux, France, where it was said their competition with local lenders depressed interest rates!

There was considerable foreign, and especially British, interest in investing in the newly independent states, but a series of defaults in 1826 and 1827 excluded much of Latin America (with the exception of Brazil) from the international capital markets until the late 1850s. In any event, the returns that foreign investors would have required to place funds in countries as politically unstable as Mexico or Peru would have made many investments unprofitable.

As a result, Latin America's international trade declined after independence. This was true even for countries such as Mexico that faced improving international prices for their products. The British, who were Latin America's major trading partner, believed that the decline in trade resulted from the deteriorating political circumstances some countries faced in the 1820s and 1830s. In 1830, Alexander Baring, of the famous merchant bankers Baring Brothers, told the House of Commons that "The Brazils, which were in a state of quiet . . . took £6,000,000 of [British] productions; Chili [*sic*], which was also in a state of quiet, £1,100,000 while Mexico, with resources equal to the Brazils took only £400,000; and Colombia only £540,000. Mexico was one of the richest and Chili one of the poorest of the new States. The truth was, that Mexico and Colombia were pressed and squeezed to death in order to maintain an unnatural military force. British merchants were plundered of their property, and the people were forced to continue in that lawless state which precluded the growth of rational institutions, and marred the civil interests of society." There were, then, both political and economic reasons for the depression of trade in the early nineteenth century, but these factors are not easily separable.

Brazil and the Spanish Caribbean were exceptions. Their ongoing participation in the international market reflected institutional continuity and the continuing purchase of African slave labor. The islands of the English Caribbean were at a disadvantage. They were simultaneously affected by the loss of a protected home market (1846–1850); by the abolition of the African slave trade in 1807, and of African slavery in 1834; and by competition from territories acquired during the Napoleonic Wars, as well as from newly powerful sugar producers such as Cuba. In general, then, the commercial expansion of Spanish America under the later Bourbon kings gave way to a lengthy retreat from the international market. Even so, vigorous promoters of trade with the new American states, such as Alexander Baring, could maintain "that the interests of [Great Britain] were involved in maintaining the independence of the new States of America."

The selections that follow explore some of these themes in greater detail. Tulio Halperín describes the long pause that intervened before the export economies of Latin America assumed their classic form after 1850, or in some cases, considerably later. David Eltis demonstrates just how powerful the impact of international trade was in shaping the slave economies of Brazil and Cuba (as well as the United States' South) as their export economies gathered momentum in the nineteenth century. Richard Salvucci considers the ways in which international politics shaped the changing dimensions of Mexican commercial policy. Héctor Lindo-Fuentes shows that for Central America, open economies alone provided a "weak foundation" for growth before complementary changes in the operation of the international market. And Paul Gootenberg describes Peru in the era "between silver and guano," explaining why Peruvians could resist the attractions of "free trade."

An Emerging Commercial Economy

TULIO HALPERÍN DONGHI

A prolific writer, Tulio Halperín Donghi is the author of *Politics, Economics and Society in the Revolutionary Period* (1975), *Reforma y disolución de los imperios ibéricos, 1750–1850* (1985), and numerous other works on the history of Argentina, Uruguay, and Latin America generally. His work emphasizes the political and economic consequences of change in the size, growth, and makeup of overseas trade. He is less interested in the internal market, whose importance has been stressed more by his colleague Carlos Sempat Assadourian.

This selection from Halperín's very influential *Historia contemporánea de América Latina* summarizes some of his principal observations on Latin America in the international economy between 1810 and 1850. Halperín's discussion of the economic shocks produced by independence in Spanish America is particularly relevant. In Mexico and Peru, a collapse in silver mining meant that the ability to import was to some extent limited, because the usual way of financing imports was by exporting silver. As a corollary, the supply of silver pesos in circulation—the basic component of the ordinary money supply—shrank in response to the demand for imports. In Mexico, Peru, and Argentina, complaints about the dislocations that this situation produced were widespread. In Lima, prices were actually about 30 percent lower by 1830 than in 1800. In other words, the integration of several of the former core economies of Spain's American empire into the Atlantic economy was by no means smooth, and the transition to liberal trade regimes was limited.

Tulio Halperín Donghi, *The Contemporary History of Latin America*. Edited and translated by John Charles Chasteen. Durham, NC: Duke University Press, 1993, pp. 79-88. Reprinted by permission.

Halperín also emphasizes the "militarization" of Spain's former colonies, a process that consumed a significant share of resources. Public finance became a matter of paying for the military, which put impossible demands on public treasuries. In Mexico, for instance, the domestic public debt began to rocket upward in the 1830s, as financiers required successive governments to recognize the debts of their predecessors before receiving access to fresh credits. The foreign debts of Argentina, Chile, Central America, Gran Colombia, Mexico, and Peru were all in default by 1830, and between 1825 and 1850, only Brazil received additional foreign loans. Relations with foreign governments, investors, and merchants all became complicated. Moreover, governments reliant on customs revenues for finance tended to discourage trade by the very act of taxing it. The overall environment was by no means conducive to the rapid expansion of internal trade. The stage was set not for the rapid and complete incorporation of Spain's former American colonies into the Atlantic economy, but for a more hesitant, piecemeal, and altogether more gradual process of transformation.

Along with the impact of fifteen years of warfare, fifteen years of being fully open to the Atlantic economy had produced a transformation no less profound and enduring. The patriots had made freedom of trade part of their revolutionary program, while the royalists had been forced to adopt a similar policy in practice because of their dependence on a British alliance. The result was a fundamental alteration in the relationship between Spanish America and the rest of the world. The international context in which the change took place conditioned the outcome. During the first half of the nineteenth century (with the exception of the two feverish years preceding the London financial collapse of 1825), no European country made large capital investments in Spanish America. Although the political turmoil of the period is cited as the reason for this omission, a look at the European economies suggests an additional explanation. Precisely during the years in question, England and the other industrializing powers of Europe produced barely enough surplus capital to cover the requirements of the first age of railroad building in the European continent and the United States.

During the first generation of Spanish American independence, the industrial economies of Europe needed a market not for their capital but for the manufactured products of their own industries.

Their main economic concern within Spanish American lands was the monopolization of trading circuits. Among the agricultural exports Spanish America could offer in return, only sugar received a priority on the European agenda. Spanish America's precious metals retained their luster, but even so, the mines did not attract sufficient outside capital to recover the levels of productivity of the late colonial period. Instead, Great Britain saturated Spanish American markets with manufactured imports as early as 1815. As other manufacturing countries, including the United States, began to enter the competition, the imagined promise of Spanish American markets sank ever deeper into red ink.

Those who lost most in these years were precisely those who had dominated the commercial system of the colonies. This group had first been weakened by the split between its Creole* and its peninsular members. Hoping to benefit from the ruin of their peninsular rivals, Creole merchants found themselves even less able to resist the onslaught of the foreign traders who rushed in next. The foreigners—especially the British merchants—were less vulnerable to the extortions of the indigent republican governments. However, most important in the decline of the Creole merchants was the collapse of their former commercial networks. Their principal trade link with Cádiz had been cut by decades of war and revolution, and the new link with London (after 1820, with Liverpool) privileged above all their new British competitors. Meanwhile, British and North American shipping crowded the nascent Spanish American merchant marines out of the sea lanes.

The European commercial conquest pushed further, into the formerly internal trade circuits between different parts of Spanish America. From Tampico to Valparaíso, British merchants began to trade directly in secondary ports that had once dealt with the outside world through primary ports like Veracruz or Lima. In only a few years, the richest prizes in Spanish American trade passed into the hands of foreigners. In her trip to Mexico in the early 1840s, Fanny Calderón de la Barca found the most impressive dwellings of interior towns already belonging to British merchants. A generation later, British surnames abounded in the upper-class families of

---

*Creoles were settlers of predominantly Spanish background born in America—American Spaniards.

Buenos Aires and elsewhere. In many ways, the domination of Cádiz had simply been exchanged for the hegemony of Liverpool.

There were important differences between the emissaries of Cádiz and those of London or Liverpool, however, and they made themselves felt strongly in the years between 1810 and 1815. Charged with finding outlets for their country's surplus industrial production, the British merchant-adventurers of this period raced aggressively into areas newly liberated from Spanish control, bringing with them a much higher volume of trade than had characterized the colonial system. At least initially, the refashioned trading network put a larger supply of money into circulation—something that the colonial merchants had been careful to avoid, since a general scarcity of currency gave them special advantages in their dealings with rural producers. Both changes constituted improvements for most Spanish Americans, but they sounded a death knell for the Creole traders, whose profits derived from strict limitations on the circulation of money and goods.

Unfortunately, the new system quickly encountered limits of its own. A depression in Europe held down the prices of Spanish American exports while, as has been previously mentioned, the real capacity of the Spanish American market to absorb manufactures proved disappointing, especially given the entry of competitors into that market after 1815. The industrial economy of Great Britain required that its trading representatives handle a relatively steady volume of manufactured products, especially textiles, a circumstance that often burdened British merchants with excessive inventories. North American traders, on the other hand, were much less driven by the need to unload an industrial surplus. They typically arrived in smaller vessels and dealt in variable stocks selected according to the fluctuating exigencies of the Spanish American market. British commercial policy therefore became increasingly rigid with the passage of time.

Despite the rigidities of the emerging commercial system, its higher volume of imports constituted a major innovation. Most of the newly imported products were inexpensive goods for a mass market, often carefully tailored to suit local Spanish American tastes. Ponchos woven in the mills of Manchester with designs imitating the looms of Pampas Indians easily undersold the local product in the Argentine hinterland. Crates of Mexican *sarapes* made in Glasgow crowded wharves alongside boxes of "Toledo" cutlery from Sheffield. Besides conquering existing markets, the early glut of manufactured imports shaped the expectations of new Spanish American consumers. A growing proportion of the total volume of European imports during this period consisted in ever-cheaper cotton fabrics for the widening market. One well-known consequence of this state of affairs was the slow and incomplete—but irrevocable—deterioration of artisan production, as in the Andean highlands, where the cotton cloth of New England gradually overwhelmed the sweatshops run with Indian labor.

Another consequence of the permanently higher volume of importation was an enduring trade imbalance and a renewed drain on the money supply. The governments of the new republics were hardly able to put legal limits on the flood of importations, even when they recognized the benefits of doing so. Given the wide market for the imported goods of the period, such limits would have been vastly unpopular. Furthermore, the pressure of landowners eager to protect their export products forced governments to depend in most cases on import tariffs for the bulk of the states' revenues. Like their colonial counterparts, the new masters of the market wanted precious metals rather than agricultural products in trade for their manufactured imports. In the Río de la Plata, cut off from the mining areas of Bolivia that once supplied its silver, the consequence was a severe reduction of the money in circulation, and even Chile, which expanded its production of silver, suffered from a similar scarcity.

Such was the emerging equilibrium of the Spanish American commercial system in the period after the wars of independence. The epoch of large foreign investments would not arrive until the second half of the nineteenth century. In the meantime, there must have been a modest, hidden flow of foreign investment as successful European merchants bought land, but this sort of investment was itself limited by the low profitability of the agricultural sector. The position of that sector had improved slightly, relative to the commercial sector, but not nearly to the degree that some had envisioned during the movements for independence. Instead, Spanish American producers had been integrated into a new international trading system that shared an important characteristic with the Spanish colonial system: it was controlled by Europeans for their own benefit. Again, the tutelage of Spain had been replaced by that of Great Britain.

The British did not achieve their hegemony without overcoming some serious competitors. Between 1815 and 1830, the main challenger was the United States. U.S. enterprises enjoyed a number of early successes, and around 1825 British consular officials in Mexico, Lima, and Buenos Aires were all sounding the alarm about the proliferation of Yankee traders. The U.S. presence was strengthened by the ostensible political affinity among fellow American republics. Unfortunately for the U.S. interests, they tended to ally themselves with the more progressive factions within Spanish American countries against the more conservative forces allied with the British, and the conservatives came out the winners almost everywhere. Soon the diplomatic representatives of the United States had the unpleasant duty of reporting the courteous indifference of Spanish American officials, who nevertheless rushed to ingratiate themselves with British diplomats. In economic terms, U.S. competition declined steadily as the new commercial networks were consolidated, and the greater flexibility of the Yankee trading style became less of an advantage as the steady fall in the prices of cotton textiles from Lancashire edged the rougher New England product out of the Spanish American market.

After 1830, France became Britain's main rival in Spanish America. French commerce was more complementary than threatening to British interests because France specialized in luxury consumer articles and in Mediterranean food products of the kind that Spain had formerly supplied, but the mere fact that a great European power maintained close ties in Spanish America presented a potential danger in the eyes of British policymakers. Fortunately for the British, French political claims, meant to affirm the country's influence, tended to miscarry and eventually dissipated the perceived menace. An early French intervention in Mexico did prove successful, but a simultaneous and more problematic involvement in the Río de la Plata obtained much smaller benefits. Both episodes served principally to alienate the sympathies with which many Spanish Americans had previously regarded France. Aggressive and unpredictable French policies were no match for the subtle, systematic imposition of British hegemony.

Despite the occasionally alarmist reports of its diplomatic representatives, Great Britain's sway over Spanish America was never really in doubt during this period. The British government used its undeniable political influence to defend the interests of its mercantile representatives (who were the object of growing unpopularity after 1815) and consolidated its privileged situation by hurrying to recognize the newly independent states and then securing in return highly advantageous treaties of friendship, commerce, and navigation. Their hegemony rested mostly on treaties, commercial superiority, and naval power, but it functioned so effectively because of the extremely restrained manner in which the British made use of their leverage. Without a lot of surplus capital to invest, the British preferred for the time being to restrict their activities to the mercantile sphere, while eschewing any deeper involvement in the local economies.

British economic dominance contrasted with former Spanish dominance in that it was accomplished without direct political control. The beneficiaries of this informal empire avoided the complication and expense of administering it. They bore no responsibility for arbitrating the violent clashes among various local interests. Instead, they left those dubious honors to the Spanish American elites and concentrated on their profit margins. They did, of course, have very well defined ideas about which policies were most advisable and displayed no inhibitions about vigorously advancing their point of view, but their goals were generally quite limited and always pursued with a keen eye to the diminishing returns of their efforts. Stubborn resistance usually brought a quick abandonment of British insistence, as their dismayed internal allies discovered in many an instance. This minimalist approach corresponded to the commercial inspirations of British policy, which originated more often among the country's merchant representatives in Spanish America than among the high policy-making circles of the Foreign Office. In general, such policies sought to maintain present advantages along with a reasonable degree of internal order. With exceptions that became increasingly rare as the century advanced, the status quo remained the cynosure of British policy. . . .

Only toward the middle of the nineteenth century did the United States begin to loom on the horizon as a contender for political supremacy in the Caribbean because of its triumph in the Mexican-American War and its tentative interest in annexing Cuba. The future influence of the United States received official recognition in the Clayton-Bulwer Treaty of 1850, an Anglo-American agreement regarding the future construction of an isthmian canal. The still-limited interests of the United States in northern Latin

America were driven by the double engines of territorial expansionism (viewed by U.S. southerners as a way to strengthen the institution of slavery) and the need to find a quicker route between the eastern United States and the gold fields of California. . . .

Of course, there existed significant contrasts between different regions within Spanish America. Despite the disruptions of war in Venezuela and the Río de la Plata, the agricultural exportations of these areas soon surpassed the most prosperous years of colonial rule. Each had inherited from the colonial period an economy already oriented toward agricultural and livestock production for the trans-Atlantic market. The advantage of having such an orientation already in place outweighed the disadvantages of political turbulence. In Peru, Bolivia, and particularly Mexico, the economic picture was dismal by contrast. The mining industries of all three had suffered tremendous destruction during the wars of independence and could not return to prewar production levels without significant investment from overseas. In the absence of that investment, Mexico's mining output declined to half of that of the last decades of colonial rule. In New Granada and Chile, a rise in livestock production for export helped compensate for the decline of the silver mines. Chile also began to export copper worth more than its silver and gold combined in the mid-1820s (though silver exports recovered first place in the 1830s).

In a striking reversal, the former marginal areas of Spanish American colonization had surpassed the old core areas of the empire in economic vitality. In 1810, exports of the Río de la Plata had amounted to a mere fifth of the value of Mexican exports, but by mid-century the two areas exported products of comparable value. Though Platine exports no longer included silver from Potosí, livestock production for export had increased tenfold. The same pattern manifested itself in a less extreme form throughout Spanish America. Without production for export or capital for innovations, most of Central America had stagnated. In Honduras and Nicaragua, the American traveler John Lloyd Stevens met ranchers who owned extensions as vast as some European provinces but who were unable to transform their land and animals into capital wealth because of their isolation from the market. Meanwhile, the central valley of Costa Rica, one of the poorest parts of colonial Central America, had established a very profitable link to that market through the cultivation of coffee. Finally, Cuba, another of the marginal areas that had entered rapid economic growth on the eve of independence, ranked with Argentina and Venezuela as one of Spanish America's most dynamic exporters in the second quarter of the nineteenth century. The moment was quite favorable for Cuba because of the disruption of sugar production in the British Antilles (where slavery had recently been abolished) and because of the commercial liberalization allowed by Spain (desperate to retain the little that remained of its empire). Between 1815 and 1850, Cuban sugar exports surged roughly from 40,000 to 200,000 tons. The Atlantic coast of Spanish America, so secondary in the imperial scheme of things until the late eighteenth century, would lead the older highland and Pacific coast areas in economic growth during much of the nineteenth century.

The newly independent Brazilian empire shared in the dynamism of the Atlantic coast economies. To begin with, the disorganization of sugar production in the British Antilles stimulated Brazilian sugar exports as it did Cuban exports, bringing a temporary return of prosperity to the sugar-growing regions along the northeast coast of Brazil. In the far south, Brazilian territory witnessed an expansion of ranching analogous to developments in the nearby Río de la Plata. Economic vitality in the north and the south created a centrifugal tendency and strained the political dominance of Rio de Janeiro, and if the Brazilian empire remained intact in the 1820s and 1830s, it was not without considerable conflict. By the 1840s, however, the rise of the coffee economy in the lands around Rio de Janeiro helped restore political and economic equilibrium and ushered in a period of stability. The Brazilian adaptation to the new political and economic order became a model often compared to the Spanish American republics as a measure of their failure. Brazil adapted more successfully partly thanks to strong continuities between the Portuguese period and the independence period. The tutelage of Portugal had always rested more lightly on its colony than had Spain's on its colonies, and the exchange of Portuguese political hegemony for British economic hegemony had taken place gradually.

Still, Brazil's transition to the new order contained some difficult contradictions. The new prosperity of the sugar economy and the rise of coffee plantations put the Brazilian government at cross-purposes with Great Britain in the matter of the slave trade. Unlike the slave regime of the southern United States, the slave population of Brazil did not reproduce itself fast enough to compensate for its high death rate, and it steadily declined without the continuous importation of enslaved Africans. Thus, the Brazilian government came under intense pressure from the sugar planters to resist British efforts at abolition of the slave trade, and, even while agreeing in theory to ban the trade, the Brazilians stubbornly protected it in practice. In some years during the early nineteenth century, traders brought in record numbers of slaves, partly because the determined British campaign against the slave trade indicated that an inevitable crisis lay ahead. While tenaciously defending the slave trade, the Brazilian government gradually gave ground in various other conflicts with the hegemonic power of Great Britain. The 1827 treaty between the two countries confirmed important concessions extracted by the British in 1810 during the French occupation of Portugal: the complete opening of the Brazilian market to goods imported from England (prohibiting any kind of protective tariff) and the retention of special courts for British residents in Brazil. As a result, Brazil overshadowed all Spanish American countries as a market for British products. The value of British goods imported into Brazil soon reached four times the value of British imports to the Río de la Plata, producing a huge trade imbalance and an inexorable drain on the money supply.

Cuba, Brazil, and the Atlantic Slave System

DAVID ELTIS

David Eltis has written a number of significant writings on slavery and the slave trade. They include "Europeans and the Rise and Fall of Slavery in the Americas: An Interpretation," *American Historical Review* (1993), and (with Lawrence C. Jennings) "Trade Between Western Africa and the Atlantic World in the Pre-Colonial Era," *American Historical Review* (1988). In this reading, Eltis helps explain why Brazil and Cuba were exceptions to

David Eltis, *Economic Growth and the Ending of the Transatlantic Slave Trade*, 1987, pp. 32–34, 37–38, 40–41, 42–43, 46. Reprinted by permission of Oxford University Press.

the pattern of slow growth that largely typified the former colonies of Spain before mid-century.

Political stability, of course, was a factor. Cuba remained a Spanish colony, and growing internal tensions over slavery notwithstanding, it could pursue economic expansion under what were, in comparison with the mainland states, relatively peaceful conditions. Brazilian independence came without bloodshed in 1822, although a number of provincial rebellions broke out between 1830 and 1850. In describing the situation in Cuba and Brazil, however, Eltis stresses access to a growing supply of slave labor created by a number of circumstances. In Cuba, for instance, administrative barriers to the employment of slave labor were reduced by the 1790s. Moreover, the outbreak of a slave revolt in St. Domingue disrupted sugar production in the 1790s and depressed the demand for slaves, which drove down prices for others who sought to employ them. The termination of the slave trade to the United States in 1807 had a similar effect. At the same time, the growing European demand for staples such as sugar and coffee made the production of these goods increasingly attractive for those with access to a labor supply, which Cuba and Brazil both possessed in the form of slaves.

An attractive feature of Eltis's explanation for the unfolding of the plantation system in the post-Napoleonic era is the idea of comparative advantage. As economists are aware, free markets allocate resources to those enterprises best able to employ them profitably. The emergence of Cuba and Brazil as major employers of slaves to produce sugar and coffee, and indeed, the shift in both economies to employing slaves only in the most profitable crops, is a clear illustration of the principle of comparative advantage. So, for instance, in Cuba, coffee production fell as sugar gained ground. In Brazil, at least over the very long run, the transformation moved in precisely the opposite direction. In each case, it was the most efficiently produced crop (or the most efficient producer of the crop) that could afford the expense that the employment of slave labor entailed. Hence the rise of Cuba and Brazil in the nineteenth century.

In the 1760s as European demand pressures began to build, almost all supplies of plantation produce came from regions controlled by five separate political powers—six if we anticipate the independence of most of British North America. In addition to what became the United States, there were the British Caribbean, the Dutch and

French West Indies and the colonies of the two Iberian powers. Although natural endowments dictated some specialization, national rivalries and the prevailing political philosophy in Europe ensured that each system pursued imperial self-sufficiency: Each national grouping of tropical colonies attempted to produce a wide range of products. By the mid-eighteenth century, the British and the French were the most successful, with the latter becoming the major supplier of Continental European markets. In the British case, first Barbados and then Jamaica became the biggest single source of sugar in the world. Before American independence the British system produced significant percentages of the world's marketed tobacco; indigo and rice were also important crops. After 1783 and the loss of the major growing areas for tobacco, indigo and rice, output in the sugar colonies became more diversified. Whereas 90 percent of Jamaican exports were sugar products in 1770, the equivalent figure in 1790 was 75 percent; in the late 1820s it was 67 percent. Coffee became a significant crop for the first time. The French, though consuming little sugar domestically, became the preeminent sugar producer in the eighteenth century. Yet a similar pattern of diversification is apparent in the French West Indies with nearly 40 percent of the exports of St. Domingue in 1767 and over 50 percent in 1775 composed of nonsugar crops such as indigo, coffee and cotton. St. Domingue, nevertheless, remained the largest sugar-producing region in the world. In Surinam, the largest of the Dutch possessions, increasing diversification of exports was also very marked after 1750.

The Iberian Americas were the least developed of all the American regions in the mid-eighteenth century. This was despite the fact that the output of the old established sugar plantations of Bahia and Pernambuco together with the newer units of the Campos region rivaled that of Jamaica. In addition, Bahian roll tobacco was sold throughout the world. The major Brazilian export in 1750, however, was still gold from the Minas Gerais: In the middle decades of the eighteenth century, the slave-labor force of this region contributed the major portion of the world's gold supply. The size of the Portuguese domestic market was such that most Brazilian produce was sold in third markets. Although roll tobacco survived because its properties were difficult to reproduce elsewhere, sugar producers of northern Brazil found it increasingly difficult to cope with the secular fall in sugar prices that continued to the 1730s. Brazilian sugar output changed little between 1650 and 1750, except for periods when war removed either British or French supplies from the European market. By 1750, moreover, gold production in the Minas Gerais had passed its peak. Of the Spanish Americas, Cuba produced hides, tobacco and a small amount of sugar, though only the latter product came from plantations. Only Venezuela, with cocoa and tobacco, produced exportable quantities of plantation products. But without major state initiatives—in the form of the financing of monopoly trading companies—it is unlikely that any Cuban sugar or Venezuelan cocoa would have been produced for export.

The Iberian regions and products were thus very much on the fringe of the developments that expanded plantation cultivation in the Americas. Moreover, the factors that seemed to have generated the rapid development of the British and French plantation systems were not about to end. France and Britain continued as the dominant European powers. The land frontiers of their possessions and their ability to acquire more appeared almost limitless. The supply of coerced labor in addition was subject to no restrictions either from without or within the African continent. Yet a hundred years later, the major features of the eighteenth-century plantation systems had largely disappeared. Three dominant plantation regions had emerged by the mid-nineteenth century: Cuba, southern Brazil and the U.S. South. Not only had none of these been of more than minor importance in the previous century, but neither France nor Britain held sovereignty over them. Indeed Cuba and southern Brazil were controlled or had recently become independent of two of the most economically backward of European countries. The product mix of the new regions, moreover, exhibited a degree of specialization unknown since the early days of the old sugar colonies. By midcentury, between 80 and 90 percent of the exports of Cuba, southern Brazil and the U.S. South were comprised of sugar, coffee and cotton, respectively. Brazil and the United States produced over half the world's output of coffee and cotton, and Cuba was responsible for one third of all sugar production. None of these products had been of much importance in these regions in 1760. The explanation of these shifts in the locus, control and product mix of the major plantation economies falls into three stages, divided chronologically by the St. Domingue revolution and the abolition of the British and U.S. slave trades in 1807. But the whole of these developments were determined to a greater or lesser degree by the structure of European economic growth.

In the generation after 1760, most plantation regions experienced prosperity. Although the British colonies expanded their output, their position relative to St. Dominigue slipped. Partly, of course, this is explained by the destructive hurricanes and independence of the mainland colonies that put U.S. supplies and provisions out of legal reach of the West Indian planter. But a more important reason was the phenomenal development of the north and west plains of St. Domingue. The largest French West Indian colony had already overtaken Jamaica in sugar output in the 1730s and established a similar position in other produce thereafter. Yet the most spectacular expansion was yet to come. In the 1780s the slave population of St. Domingue almost doubled and slave imports averaged thirty thousand per annum in the last years of the decade. The French colony had come to overshadow Jamaica in the production of all types of plantation produce, just as the latter's sugar production had overtaken that of Barbados earlier in the century. Aggregate slave imports into the Americas reached an all-time decadal high between 1781 and 1790. Yet the central fact of the period 1770–91 was that despite massive expansion of output in most plantation regions, peacetime prices of sugar, cotton, indigo and tobacco continued to rise. Clearly the increase in demand exceeded the increase in supply, and demand pressures previously felt by non-British and non-French areas only in time of war, now became steady and permanent. . . .

For the British, Portuguese and Spanish colonies, the French colonial collapse meant a huge boost in demand for produce and probably, too, a lower African price for slaves. The demise of the French slave trade was mainly responsible for the lower slave prices and this was due mainly to the war with Britain that began in 1793. But there can be no doubt that the expansion of the non-French areas in the 1790s was due in the main to the same European developments that had triggered their earlier growth. The British, Portuguese and Spanish who had produced, respectively, 36.7, 6.6 and 6.3 percent of the sugar imported by the North Atlantic countries in 1787 increased their market share steadily thereafter. British colonial and Brazilian shares of the raw cotton market jumped by 50 percent between 1786–87 and 1796–1800, and the redistribution of coffee production was only slightly less dramatic. A more important point is that the markets that were thus redistributed were growing at an unprecedented rate. In the twenty years down to 1805, British sugar consumption rose 80 percent and cotton imports quadrupled despite prices that increased in real terms. Even without the St. Domingue rebellion, the 1790s would have been a prosperous decade for non-French plantations in the Americas. . . .

Beginning in 1805 first British and then U.S. abolition of the slave trade destroyed the homogeneity. British and American plantations inevitably faced higher labor costs in the wake of abolition, given the expansion of demand for plantation produce. But in the American case a very high rate of natural increase in the slave population, beginning early in the previous century, greatly mitigated the economic impact of abolition. Indeed if the same rate of natural decrease that existed for Caribbean slave populations had held for U.S. slaves, then nineteenth-century slave trade to the United States would have had to have matched the free-migrant flow from Europe for the slave population to have reached the level it did in 1860. The Caribbean epidemiological environment and the sex and age structure of the British slave population ensured that the slave populations of areas that had imported heavily in the years preceding abolition would decline. These same factors also ensured that when slave populations did begin to increase, they would do so slowly. In the generation after slave-trade abolition, when the American slave population doubled, its British counterpart declined by at least 10 percent and by even more in the colonies with the greatest potential for increased output. British planters showed considerable ingenuity in the deployment and organization of their labor forces, so that production levels, at least for sugar, were maintained or increased slightly. But British producers were now in a straitjacket. The slave price differential between the Spanish Caribbean, on the one hand, and the British and American plantation areas, on the other, that had existed in the eighteenth century reappeared, but this time to the advantage of the Spanish producers . . . .

The inability of British planters to expand their output in response to burgeoning world markets has already been discussed. It was due not so much to higher labor costs as to the complete unavailability of free labor at a price at which a plantation could operate profitably. Markets that might have been filled by British producers were now open to the Brazilians and Cubans. British sugar consumption increased at a mean annual rate of just under 1.5 percent between 1805 and 1825. As this was the slowest secular growth in the British market between 1650 and 1900, it seems likely that the rest of the North Atlantic market was growing more quickly at this time. British West Indian sugar production was growing at only 0.5 percent per year on average between 1801–05 and 1821–25, though its rate of growth throughout the 1820s allowed it to keep pace with consumption in Britain at least. Brazilian and Cuban producers filled much of the resulting gap in non-British markets as their output expanded at from double to quadruple the British rates between 1805 and 1830. The different degrees of processing in sugar exports make comparisons difficult but, by any reasonable measurement, it is clear that the British sugar colonies continued to produce more sugar than both Brazil and Cuba together until the final abolition of British slavery itself in 1833. The pattern in coffee was similar. Exports of coffee from Cuba grew at the phenomenal rate of 13 percent per year in the first two decades of the century, and at a yearly average of nearly 15 percent during the 1820s. Production surpassed that of the British West Indies, which changed little in the same period. The strongest growth came after British abolition of the slave trade rather than before, even though the shift of growers from St. Domingue to Cuba had already taken place by 1808. Brazilian competition, which eventually contributed to the decline of the Cuban industry, became significant only after 1810. Although Brazilian output expanded even faster than its Cuban counterpart, it did not exceed British and Cuban production until the mid-1820s.

The natural advantages of Cuba and southern Brazil in the production of sugar and coffee may have outweighed those of Demerara, Jamaica and Trinidad, but there were few signs of it before 1807 or for several years after. As we have seen, the remarkably flexible response of British planters and slaves meant that as late as the 1820s the British were selling sugar profitably in the same markets as the Cubans despite having higher labor costs. Yet even in the absence of the 1833 Emancipation Act, this situation might not have continued. In the long run Iberian access to Africa meant that after 1805 the Iberian and British planter simply did not compete on equal terms. At the very least, planters in the Iberian Americas could have asked for nothing better from the British government (except perhaps to leave their own slave trade untouched) than to abolish first the slave trade and then slavery in the British colonies . . . .

The structure of the American plantation systems and their relationship with Africa was thus profoundly altered in the generation
before 1810. Of the six major systems of the 1780s, only one, the
Spanish, did not have free access to African-born labor. Thirty years
later the biggest of these systems, the French, had been reduced to
fragments of territory and slave imports of a few thousand a year
smuggled in during the decade after the Napoleonic wars. A second
system, the Dutch, had been partially absorbed by a third, the
British, and neither system was allowed even illicitly introduced
slaves after 1807. Indeed in the Dutch case few Africans were introduced after 1795. A fourth, that of the United States, had also insti-
tuted abolition and although demographic trends provided a natural
substitute, product specialization quickly ensured little direct competition between this system and the two others that were relatively
free of restrictions on their supply of labor. Of the six systems,
therefore, only two, the Spanish and the Portuguese, had free access
to Africa in 1810, and this access did not remain completely free for
very long. Treaties between England and first Portugal, then Spain
and next Brazil had the effect of making illegal the traffic to Bahia
and north Brazil in 1815, the Cuban trade in 1820 and the trade to
southern Brazil ten years later. But the Africans continued to arrive.
There are, thus, two underlying causes of the rapid expansion of the
slave systems of the Iberian Americas in the nineteenth century. One
was obviously the accelerating demand for produce, behind which
lay the economic and demographic growth of the North Atlantic lit-
toral, in particular Great Britain. The other was the destruction or
shackling of the non-Iberian systems that, without such restraints,
would have claimed much larger shares of the world produce market than they, in fact, did. Because antislavery was responsible for
these restraints and was itself linked to the ideological ramifications
of economic growth, industrialization gave a double stimulus to
slavery in Cuba and Brazil.

Texas, "Tyrants," and Trade with Mexico

RICHARD SALVUCCI

The opening of the Latin American economies to international trade in the early nineteenth century depended critically on a number of specific domestic circumstances, both political and economic. There was no generally applicable model, and certainly no rush to free trade. Moreover, the decision to adopt liberal trade regimes was by no means imposed from without on unwitting and unwilling victims. Richard Salvucci, author of *Textiles and Capitalism in Mexico: An Economic History of the Obrajes* (1987), argues for instance that Mexican trade with the United States occurred within a thoroughly politicized context. Early nineteenth-century Mexican politicians believed that liberalizing trade with the United States invited political pressure, territorial aggression, and the inevitable compromise of Mexican sovereignty. The example of Texas in the 1830s influenced their thinking. The Texas rebellion had a measurable impact on patterns of Mexican trade with the United States and Great Britain down through the outbreak of the Mexican War. As a result, most Mexican regimes remained, at best, ambivalent toward the idea of liberalizing trade with the United States. For much of the early nineteenth century, Mexico resisted unqualified integration into the international market. Expansive commercial interests in the United States often assumed that threats, intimidation, and in the final instance, open force were required to induce the Mexicans to behave "fairly" toward them. Mexicans were, in this view, indifferent to the self-evident benefits of freer trade, and hence disinterested in peace, progress, advancement, and republican government.

So international trade became an early and enduring source of conflict between Mexico and the United States. Commercial treaties, tariffs, and import restrictions were a source of controversy between the two and remained so for much of the nineteenth century. Mexicans often defined national autonomy and sovereignty as freedom from the entangling consequences of trade with

Richard J. Salvucci, "The Origins and Progress of U.S. Mexican Trade, 1825–1884: Hoc opus, hic labor est," *Hispanic American Historical Review,* 71:4 (1991), pp. 697–698, 711–720.

the United States. Observers from the United States were quick to define Mexicans as financially, economically, and consequently, morally irresponsible. There were respites from this pattern of contention and liberalized trade between the two nations. But for both political and economic reasons, Mexico remained in its dealings with the United States sometimes exclusionist, often protectionist, and inevitably wary. Skepticism about the benefits of liberalized trade dampened Mexico's enthusiasm for opening markets, even when favorable international price trends might have suggested more rather than less trade. It was not until the 1880s, and the opening of rail links with the United States, that a rapid expansion of trade and commerce between the two nations got underway.

The economic and commercial history of early national Mexico remains very much a mystery, the contributions of John Coatsworth, Donald Stevens, Barbara Tenenbaum, Guy Thomson, David Walker, and numerous Mexican scholars notwithstanding. In part, the problem is one of finding, collating, and interpreting statistics that are frequently difficult, conjectural, or contradictory. But it is also a question of knowing where to start; of deciding what is important; and of creating a framework within which statistics and other economic data assume coherence, consistency, and meaning, even in the presence of incomplete information.

A likely point of departure is foreign trade. It is clear from the work of Stevens, Tenenbaum, and Thomson that foreign trade is central to discussions of political change, capital movements, indebtedness, and commercial policy. Foreign trade was nearly at the heart of early national political economy. But the composition, evolution, and effects of foreign trade are by no means well known, much less undisputed. Tenenbaum links the fragility of the fiscal system, and indirectly of federalism itself, almost entirely to the cyclical variability of trade and tariffs. Stevens, on the other hand, discerns a politicized economic cycle and reverses cause and effect, concluding that "politicians [in Mexico] did not merely respond to economic cycles, but caused them." Clearly then, examining foreign trade is a means of understanding issues that largely defined the existence, character, and viability of the Mexican state in the early national period. "Sin hacienda, no hay estado," as a publication of the day remarked.

Yet a study of Mexico's foreign trade in the early nineteenth century is also necessarily an analysis of its commercial policy. And commercial policy was, and is, a weapon. It was, perhaps, uniquely effective against the pressures that both Great Britain and the United States exerted on Mexico, for the Mexican market was an object of competition between them, and competition brings leverage. Mexico employed the weapon, sometimes successfully and sometimes less so, but always in reaction to enormous pressures on its sovereignty. In Mexican eyes, the flag followed trade. . . .

Texas dominated the political economy of the first cycle [of Mexico's independent history]. Its trauma diverted Mexican trade toward Great Britain, whose role as a potential counterweight to U.S. territorial designs on Mexico ended only with annexation and the Mexican War. The theme appears in modern Mexican scholarship and pervades the writings of men as different as Alamán and Carlos María de Bustamante. The message is clear: the flag follows trade. Trading with the United States brings their merchants, and their merchants bring trouble. "They are the true sons of Englishmen," wrote Bustamante, "whose example in India they remember and emulate. Merchants financed the invading expedition. Once their company had gotten hold of the land, they turned it over to the crown, which installed a government and set millions of Indians groaning under a slavery enforced by bayonets." . . .

Alamán's point was much the same. "Instead of armies, battles, and invasions, which raise such uproar and generally prove abortive, [the United States] use means which, considered separately, seem slow, ineffectual, and sometimes palpably absurd, but which united, and in the course of time, are certain and irresistible." And what were these means? The list was a long one, but the first Alamán mentioned was "commercial negotiations."

To be sure, Mexico had never trusted U.S. commercial ambitions. In 1829, Secretary of State Martin Van Buren termed Mexico's dilatory consideration of a treaty of reciprocity a "mistaken policy . . . unfriendly to the commercial prospect of the United States." Mexico regarded the United States "with a degree of indifference and suspicion as extraordinary as it was to be regretted." Negotiation over the treaty, which had begun in 1826, dragged on until 1832. And even then, "the first attempts of our adventurous citizens [were] burdened by the imposition of prohibitive duties . . . [in] Mexican ports."

The tariff, then, was Mexico's weapon of choice. Before the War of 1847, Mexico repeatedly adjusted its coverage and level, most notably in 1829, 1837, and 1842–43. In theory, the tariffs covered a variety of articles, but in practice their target was finished cottons, the industry that Mexican industrialists sought most strongly to protect. Things started badly in 1825, with allegations of discriminatory duties on U.S. cottons, and by 1827 rising duties had driven U.S. exports sharply down. Matters worsened in 1829, and U.S. merchants in Veracruz warned that the new duty's "pernicious influence . . . has annihilated the reviving spirit of commercial enterprise." The U.S. consul concurred. When pressed, Lucas Alamán, then secretary of home and foreign relations, promised relief. But his suggesting that repeal of the duty on coarse cottons would pass the Mexican Senate "without the slightest opposition" was simply bad faith on Alamán's part.

Much worse was in store. In the continuing wake of the Texas crisis, the tariff was again revised. Although some duties were reduced in 1837, the new schedule prohibited (effective March 1838) ordinary cottons and woolens, cotton yarn and thread, and ready-to-wear clothing. In late 1842, duties on goods otherwise permitted rose 30 to 50 percent. The Tariff of 1843 reiterated the prohibitions of 1837 but added raw cotton and coarse woolens to a list that included at least sixty articles "embracing most of the necessaries of life and far the greater portion of [U.S.] products and fabrics." As the U.S. consul in Veracruz remarked, "no cotton goods can be imported less than 25 and 30 threads [per quarter square inch] which comprises that very kind of good suited and worn by the poor and middling classes of the community." Here was a recipe for reviving the moribund *obrajes* of the colonial regime.

The prohibitions were murderously effective. Before 1838, finished cottons were 30 to 40 percent of domestic U.S. exports. Once the Tariffs of 1837 and 1842 had taken hold, the share of cottons fell to only 16 percent (see accompanying table). A small market for cotton twist, yarn, and thread was annihilated as well. "[Mexico's] commerce would be infinitely important to us," said the U.S. minister in 1842, "but for this unfortunate Texan war, which has caused much injury to the United States."

Share of Finished Cottons in U.S. Domestic Exports to Mexico

Years	Share[a]	Standard deviation
1825/26–1829/30	.338	.125
1830/31–1837/38	.414	.094
1838/39–1846/47	.162	.084
1847/48–1852/53	.235	.133
1853/54–1855/56	.067	.021
1856/57–1859/60	.108	.071
1868/69–1871/72	.058	.005
1872/73–1879/80	.131	.080

[a]Defined as the sum of plain and colored cottons divided by all domestic exports. All shares are figured in current prices.

SOURCE: Computed from the annual "Statements of [Foreign] Commerce and Navigation of the United States," 1825/26–1883/84.

In late 1845, a bill pending in the Chamber of Deputies would have admitted cotton and cotton manufactures on better terms. Seven percent of customs duties would indemnify cotton growers and manufacturers for their losses to foreign competition. The bill failed; the tariff scheduled to go into effect in February 1846 was as restrictive as its predecessors. But the war intervened, and Mexican ports were placed under blockade.

The U.S. consul in Veracruz was no doubt correct when he observed in late 1845 that "Mexico never since she has been a Nation has been in so wretched a State." But wretched is not powerless. Although an amalgam of economic nationalism and opportunism, Mexican policy nevertheless rested on the law of demand. This was the nation's best weapon.

In the long run, Mexico's strategy did not and probably could not have prevented the loss of Texas, New Mexico, and California to the United States. But in the short run it was hardly irrational. High tariffs satisfied the demand for protection that manufacturers pressed so insistently on the Mexican Congress and mollified other vital (and volatile) constituencies as well. And, indeed, trade with the United States remained small, much to the chagrin of those who had expected great things of the Mexican market. In the early days of the First Republic, newspapers in the United States hailed

Guadalupe Victoria as another George Washington. By 1845, the comparisons drawn were altogether less flattering.

A final observation. In the very short run, large fluctuations in trade occurred from year to year. Some were simply random, and not all are easily or equally explicable. Yet contemporaries understood the link between political stability and sustained growth. As one anonymous essayist put it: "The mere rumor of a revolution is pernicious. . . . Agriculture falls off, commerce is all but paralyzed, and silver shipments cease because the roads are probably not safe. In short, the citizens are in arms, and all is in disorder. These are the necessary and immediate consequences of the very rumor, more or less substantiated, of the next revolution." Uncertainty dominated yearly, and daily, affairs.

Historians of the United States once called their Civil War the "irrepressible conflict." No one familiar with relations between the United States and Mexico in the 1840s could conclude that the Mexican War was any less "irrepressible." U.S. ambitions and Mexican nationalism were mutually exclusive. Indeed, the drive to commercial and territorial expansion characteristic of U.S. foreign policy in the 1840s has been termed "manifest design" by a historian who argues that this expansion was neither accidental nor providential. In the long run, Mexico's defeat (and the annexation of Texas) implied a permanent increase in the U.S. market and a sweeping reorientation of Mexico's trade. . . .

Still, none of this happened overnight. Mexico's defeat by no means meant that the United States could appropriate a larger share of the Mexican market at will. In the short run, the spike in finished cottons sent to Mexico in 1847/48 did not and could not last (see table). It reflected the administration of a war tariff by U.S. troops in the occupied ports of Tampico and Veracruz.

Mexico still had commercial weapons, and the demand for protection remained strong. Thus, by the early 1850s, the old complaint was again heard. The United States could expect little from Mexico "whilst the system of prohibitions is observed." Meanwhile, the United States brought new territorial pressures to bear during negotiations over the Treaty of the Mesilla in 1853. James Gadsden, the U.S. minister, wanted Sonora and Chihuahua as well but did not get them. Nor did he get commercial concessions, whatever his original interest in them may have been.

Indeed, after the Treaty of the Mesilla, the Mexican government once again restricted U.S. exports, much as it had done after the Texas rebellion in 1835, and a booming postwar market for U.S. finished cottons all but collapsed (see table). By late 1854, the consul in Veracruz could write, "Santa Anna's policy destroys commerce, particularly that of the United States." In a later dispatch he quotes Gadsden, who minced no words. "I had contemplated . . . [directing] the Secretary of State's attention to the entire Santa Anna Commercial Code—so embarrassing, destructing [sic] and offensive to all trade and intercourse with Mexico—in the hope of convincing him of the necessity of getting rid of the Brigand [Santa Anna]." "Nothing," concluded U.S. Consul Pickett, "can be more corrupt, false, unequal, and generally pernicious than the entire Mexican commercial system."

The sources of this vitriol were two: "the" Tariff of 1853 and the Commercial Code of 1854. In practice, four "national" tariffs were in force in 1853, plus state and regional levies in Guadalajara and Monterrey. "How many more there may be in different sections of the country I shall not attempt to record," wrote the consul in Veracruz. Nor was the Commercial Code much better (or worse). "[O]ne might as well attempt a digest of the laws of the Meades [sic] and Persians or an abridgment of the Chinese Encyclopaedia as a codification of all the imperious arbitrary *dicta* of the absconded Mexican solon [Santa Anna]."

To the United States, all was chaos. Which tariff applied or to whom duties should be paid was not clear. "Merchants are even now continually imposed on and openly robbed under one or the other of them." This view was not unique to foreign observers. Mexican historians, too, shudder at the "fiscal disorder" that the declining Santanista dictatorship encouraged.

But why should Mexicans educated in the legacies of Guadalupe Hidalgo and the Mesilla assume that open trade with the United States was beneficial? Had it ever been? Its desirability was an axiom only in the minds of U.S. officials, who since the days of Poinsett had repeatedly complained that Mexico impeded trade. James Gadsden was no worse when he concluded, "Let us labor to kill [these barriers to trade] outright and to secure guarantees against their resurrection." Mexico's desire for autonomy (or, indeed, its definition of sovereign interests) figures nowhere in his thoughts.

Santa Anna, on the other hand, had long played cat and mouse with the United States. He understood its interest in enlarging trade and held it at bay as he picked U.S. pockets. "[The] Tariff is not a rigid law in the Republic. . . . His Most Serene Highness [Santa Anna] violates it constantly by selling exclusive privileges," observed the U.S. consul in Veracruz. By misdirecting, stalling, and confounding, Santa Anna's "chaos" forced merchants to disclose how much they were willing to pay to do business. This may have been dishonest and even inefficient in a broader economic sense, but it was an effective means of extracting rents from U.S. merchants and of restraining their enthusiasm for Mexico. True enough, Santa Anna plundered the state. But his odd ethic was shared by principled idealists whose instincts for personal, political, and national survival were equally indistinguishable. Moreover, Santa Anna displayed a studied ambivalence toward foreign trade. Waddy Thompson, the U.S. minister to Mexico from early 1842 through early 1844, portrayed him as leaning toward autarchy: "[Mexico] had no need of foreign commerce. . . . [It produced] all the necessaries of life."

The Ayutla movement of 1855 represented, in this context, a shift of substantial proportions. The Tariff of 1856, which permitted the volume of exports to Mexico to grow, was its proximate result. Finished cottons, always a sensitive indicator of the strength of protection, gained ground, and in time their share in exports recovered from the sickening collapse of 1853/54 (see table). Broadcloth, timbers, ready-made clothing, and raw cotton all disappeared from the index of prohibitions. Nominal duties on finished cottons fell by an astounding 70 percent and were lower in 1856 than at any time since 1845. By one estimate, the implicit index of protection on goods from the United States was about 30 percent, an extraordinarily low figure by historical standards.

As a harbinger of Liberal (and liberal) capitalism, the Ayutla movement embraced the national ambitions and possibilities of a bourgeoisie long frustrated by civil unrest. Their notions of growth stressed the expansion of demand rather than the control of supply, a modernizing attitude altogether different from the vague neomercantilism of the later Bourbons and their successors. Witness the words of Guillermo Prieto, who assumed the treasury portfolio in 1855: "The faith I have in free trade is the faith I have in all sublime manifestations of liberty."

Different, too, was their notion of the political economy of trade. The upswing in exports from the United States that would characterize the third cycle (1867/68–1883/84) marks the end of repeated cycles of annexation and commercial resistance. Better to yield markets than territory, dollars than dominion. Matías Romero put it succinctly: "The best means of impeding annexation is to open the country to the United States . . . with the objective of making annexation unnecessary and even undesirable. . . ."

There is, however, a final point. Repeated civil disturbances were disruptive and costly. Foreign conflict may bring prosperity, but enduring domestic crises do not. During the final days of Santa Anna, the U.S. consul in Veracruz noted that "the *Pronunciados* (Revolutionists) [have] cut off all communication with [Mexico City and] . . . the telegraph has long since been destroyed. . . . The Rebels are determined to seize the public moneys." So, too, in 1858 with the outbreak of the War of the Reform: "commerce and business [were] completely prostrate, and silver could not be shipped out through Veracruz."

The costs of remaining on a nearly permanent war footing were severe. Peasants pressed into armed service could not plant or harvest, a major source of disruption to an agrarian economy. Moving armies around the countryside required huge numbers of horses, mules, and oxen to drag artillery and to carry supplies. . . . This was one of the ways in which persistent instability reduced productivity in nineteenth-century Mexico, and its effects are especially clear from examining patterns of trade with the United States.

El Salvador from Indigo to Coffee

HÉCTOR LINDO-FUENTES

In *Spanish Central America: A Socioeconomic History, 1520– 1720* (1973), Murdo MacLeod points to a number of continuing themes in the history of Central America. For instance, MacLeod

---

Héctor Lindo-Fuentes, *Weak Foundations. The Economy of El Salvador in the Nineteenth Century, 1821–1898*, pp. 99, 102–107, 119–123 with abridgments. Copyright © 1990 The Regents of the University of California. Reprinted by permission of the publisher.

writes that "the economic history of sixteenth-century Central America can best be described as a desperate search for a key to wealth from exports," at the same time that he points to Central America's "basically Pacific orientation" (pp. 375, 387). As a response to the depression of the seventeenth century, MacLeod writes, "New World entrepreneurs were only too glad . . . to forsake their erstwhile autonomy, an autonomy of stagnation . . . and to become dependent parts of an expanding world market" (p. 389). With equal assurance, Héctor Lindo-Fuentes writes, "The expansion of the export economy financed and shaped the organization of the Salvadoran state." The development of commercial activity along the Pacific Coast following the California Gold Rush, and the establishment of steamer service by the Panama Railroad Company led to an economic expansion that intensified pressure on Indian lands, much as did the indigo boom of 1610–1630. El Salvador had long been an "open economy."

But openness was not enough. Once again, particular circumstances mattered. An important element in the expansion of the Latin American commodity trade in the nineteenth century was the sizable reduction in transportation costs. For example, Atlantic freight rates fell about 25 percent between the 1820s and the 1840s, and would fall another 20 percent by the 1860s. In El Salvador, Lindo-Fuentes emphasizes, falling transportation costs changed relative prices and made the production of export goods far more attractive. Indigo gradually gave way to coffee. And there was a short-lived cotton boom in the 1860s, as the cotton famine produced by the Civil War in the United States caused prices offered for the staple in Great Britain to skyrocket.

In short, some of the features one associates with dependency thinking, especially the pervasive impact of commercialized export agriculture on the social and production structures of a small, open economy, may be found in Lindo-Fuentes' discussion of El Salvador in the early nineteen century. Yet here the process of incorporation had had a much longer history, and its essential characteristics were to a certain extent already fixed by the middle of the colonial period.

The expansion of the export economy financed and shaped the organization of the Salvadoran state. El Salvador created itself as an independent nation in an environment of increasing openness to the outside world. Key internal decisions were responses to developments taking place thousands of miles away: gold diggers in California and railroad builders in Panama changed the direction of Salvadoran roads, a distant war in the United States turned everybody's attention to cotton production, indigo planters became coffee planters. As international trade changed the face of the nation, subsistence agriculture played an increasingly smaller secondary role. Production was meant for the market, all land had to become a commodity, and all labor had to be up for sale. El Salvador was a small country; it had no place to hide from the forces of the market. . . .

External Trade

Before the Gold Rush opened new opportunities, exports per capita were relatively modest; they amounted to less than two pesos in 1855. In less than four decades they had increased more than fourfold. Undoubtedly the opening of the markets was significant. At the middle of the century the main export product was indigo. In 1855 it accounted for 86.30 percent of Salvadoran exports. Other exports lagged far behind; they were, in order of importance: hides (4.14 percent), tobacco (3.64 percent), balsam (2.83 percent), and much smaller amounts of silver, rebozos, sugar, coffee, and other minor items. The data available for this period only include products exported by sea and do not take into account the considerable trade that took place over the borders, in particular the trade through Belize, which was still important and included a substantial amount of indigo. In 1856 the British consul reported that about 32 percent of the indigo crop was exported via Guatemala and Honduras. The position of indigo as the prime export was unquestionable. By the 1870s indigo exports were being seriously challenged by a powerful newcomer: coffee. It was a gradual but steady process; in 1874 indigo exports were, for the first time, less than half of total exports, even though the number of pounds exported was higher than in 1855. Coffee exports, which had begun in 1855, reached 35 percent of total exports in 1874 and 80 percent in 1892.

The development of trade with the rest of the world was possible thanks to changes in transportation. Lower freights, shorter routes, and better shipping services opened new possibilities. In the early 1850s indigo exports to England could follow two routes. They could either be shipped from one of the Pacific ports and go around Cape Horn or be sent by land to Belize and then shipped to

England. In 1852 it took from 110 to 150 days for vessels following the Cape Horn route to reach England. The Belize route took, with good luck, somewhat less time (84 to 115 days). Goods had to be taken from El Salvador to Lake Izabal by mule, and then they were shipped to Belize and transshipped to Liverpool. The table shows the costs in time and money involved in this route. It was three times more expensive to take goods from El Salvador to Belize than from Belize to Liverpool.

The situation started to change with the inauguration of the steamship service between Central America and California in 1854 and the Panama railroad in 1855. Already in 1858 a "considerable portion of the indigo crop" was exported by steamer via Panama. The Panama Railroad Company and later the Pacific Mail Steamship Company offered through-bills of lading from Central American ports to Liverpool, including all the costs involved in crossing the Isthmus by railroad and transshipping of goods. In 1859 the cost of shipping a 150-pound seroon of indigo by steamer to Liverpool via Panama was six pesos, less than half of the cost of shipping via Belize seven years earlier. Moreover, the time of the trip was reduced to two months, or almost in half. Ships operating the Cape Horn route had to cut prices to remain competitive. Given the high interest rates that prevailed at the time, the long duration of the route (five months in 1860) was a serious problem for exporters who had to wait for months before selling their products. By 1860 freights for the service around the Cape were a little less than

Costs of Transporting 150 pounds of Indigo from El Salvador to England in 1853

	Pesos		Days
El Savador–Izabal	7		40
Izabal–Belize	1		5
Belize–England	2	4r.	60
Transshipment			9
Taxes and Commissions	1	6r.	
Total	12	2r.	114

SOURCE: *La Gaceta*, January 21, 1853.

half that for the Panama route. A comparison between both routes taking into account interest rates and insurance costs shows that the Cape Horn route managed to remain competitive with lower prices. In less than ten years Salvadoran producers saw freights and shipping time cut in half and much more regular shipping services. The reduction of time between shipment and sale had economic advantages beyond the savings in interest. *La Gaceta* printed an insightful analysis of the problem:

> Against this [freight] difference it is necessary to keep in mind the loss of opportunities in the market, about three months during the best part of the year, besides keeping funds idle and, as a result, loss of interests, difference in market prices when the goods arrive and other considerations that have some importance.

Transportation costs did not fall as much as they could have, partly because of high demand for the services of the Panama railroad and the monopolistic practices of the company that ran it. A former employee of the company that built and operated the railroad explained the rate policies of his company with remarkable candor:

> These rates, said Colonel Center to me, long afterwards, were intended to be, to a certain extent prohibitory, until we could get things in shape. As soon as we were on our own feet and ready for business we could, as I wrote the President, gracefully reduce our charges to within reasonable limits. For it's always pleasing to the public to have prices come down rather than rise.
>
> To his surprise, these provisional rates were adopted; and what is more they remained in force for more than twenty years. It was found as easy to get large rates as small and thus, without looking very much to the future, this goose began to lay golden eggs with astonishing extravagance.*

The contribution of changes in transportation costs to economic growth during the nineteenth century is a well-established theme in the literature. In the case of El Salvador it is tempting to

---

*Tracy Robinson, *Panama 1806–1907* (New York: The Star and Herald Company, 1907), p. 24.

establish a parallel between the effect of drastic freight changes experienced by Salvadoran producers in the 1850s and the benefits derived from the construction of railroads in other countries. There are analytical differences that need to be taken into account. Freight changes were not due to an investment project carried out within the country; therefore the analysis is not really a project-evaluation problem. It is more a change in consumer surplus derived from a change in an international price. A simple and inaccurate way of calculating it would be by calculating the cost of transporting the 1865 crop via Belize and comparing it to the cost of transporting the same crop via Panama. The difference, that is, the social savings due to changes in freight rates, is an amount of 70,635.53 pesos, 5.1 percent of the value of indigo and coffee exports in 1865. This figure is clearly an upper bound since it does not take into account that the demand for shipping services would have been less at higher rates. Five percent of total exports could not have meant much in terms of the total national income. Moreover, the government subsidized Panama Railroad steamers at a rate of 8,000 pesos per year. It is clear that although the decrease in transportation costs was important, its overall significance should not be overstated. El Salvador did benefit from lower freight rates and more regular shipping services, but the changes took place at the margin. It seems that their most significant effect was not in expanding the national income but in altering its structure. Lower transportation costs made export activities more attractive relative to other productive activities such as handicrafts and food production. A trend that began timidly during the late colonial period, the expansion of the export sector, was greatly reinforced. It was irreversible.

Moreover, the change in trade routes was not completed overnight. Since the Panama Railroad was a monopoly with a very inelastic supply, it was able to operate at capacity charging very high rates. This means that it left an unsatisfied demand and that the rates were high enough for the other routes to be able to operate. The Izabal route, which had serious problems because of the long stretches of land transportation involved, was still very much alive in 1864 when indigo was exported "in great amounts by the port of Izabal in the Republic of Guatemala." It is remarkable that the new Panama route did not displace an alternative that involved traveling over roads that were unsafe, uncomfortable, expensive, and slow. The Cape Horn route was not abandoned either. It was able to compete with lower prices until the opening of the Panama Canal.

The increase in trade opened up opportunities to commercial and financial intermediaries, and a few British and American firms opened branches in El Salvador to take advantage of them. The extent of their influence on the economy is not well known today. One of their roles was to provide information about changes in the international market of the products exported by the country. The British firm Kerferd Sinclair and Company published a column in *La Gaceta* in which it gave the London prices of the main commodities. It also offered its services as credit intermediary in foreign operations and bought indigo, coffee, sugar, and cotton. The firm Guillermo A. Knoepfel of New York offered a great variety of services; an advertisement said that the company,

> will attend promptly and efficiently every order received, be it for stationery, printing, wallpaper . . . buy or hire ships, collect dividends, wills, debts. . . .

The other side of international trade, imports, is harder to analyze. Official data on imports is less reliable than the data on exports since the former paid taxes while export products paid rather minimal duties. Moreover, official trade figures give the impression that the balance of trade was always positive, something that is contradicted by the presence of outflows of specie in certain years. Imports (as well as exports) were valued at official prices that had nothing to do with market prices, and that remained the same over time. This has the advantage that the series reflect only changes in quantities and not in prices, but it says nothing about the balance of payments. It is important to keep in mind that since imports paid high taxes, there was a strong incentive to hide imports or to make "special arrangements" with customs officials who were not always above corrupt practices.

Nonetheless, there are certain trends that are clear from the data. The most important category of imports was, by far, textiles. During the second half of the century they accounted for shares of total exports between 53.17 percent in 1877 and 33 percent in 1889. The share of capital goods, by contrast, never reached 3 percent. Luxury goods, widely defined as nonessential consumer goods, varied between 12 and 31 percent, the higher figures belonging to the end of the century. Although it would be hard to say that the members of the Salvadoran elite indulged in extravagant displays of conspicuous consumption (their luxuries being rather modest by the standards of the Porfirian elite in Mexico, for example), it is also hard to find anything in the products imported that could contribute to the long-term development of the country. Even more, the high imports of textiles made it impossible to develop a local textile industry even though the country had the capacity to produce cotton.

International trade had already become an economic activity linked to all aspects of the Salvadoran economy. The dependence on the Guatemalan merchants that had prevailed at the beginning of the century disappeared. Before the development of the new trade routes, the use of the Guatemalan ports of the Atlantic was a necessity, but by the 1860s their use was a matter of choice. The indigo fairs became commercial events where exporters and importers, important businessmen, and local producers and traders met. As the economy began to grow, the links between the national and international economy became stronger. The new emphasis on coffee production was to become the key link to the international economy. . . .

From Indigo to Coffee

The transition from indigo to coffee was gradual: indigo production remained over a million pounds until the end of the century, even though prices were falling. The introduction of artificial dyes was slow. Up until 1860 the textile industry had little use for artificial dyes. The first aniline, mauveine, was not discovered until 1856. Other anilines were introduced throughout the century, but none of them was a close substitute for indigo; synthetic indigo was not introduced until 1897. By then coffee was already the main export product of El Salvador. Total coffee exports were growing but not necessarily at the expense of indigo production; much of it was net growth. Coffee production was growing faster than the population whereas indigo declined very slowly. Part of the growth was possible thanks to the introduction of new land into cultivation. The government's active sale of terrenos baldíos and the fact that land prices remained fairly stable support this hypothesis. Moreover, change in transportation costs made production for exports more attractive; resources previously used in food production and other activities were diverted. Still, if more resources were to be devoted to exports, a choice had to be made between coffee and indigo, the only viable exports.

The incentives for shifting from one product to the other were varied. At the beginning of the process, prices were not the main incentive; between 1848 and 1869 the ratio of coffee to indigo prices in the London market was decreasing. Transportation costs, by contrast, offer a more attractive explanation since they experienced a sharp decline after the opening of the Panama Railroad in 1855. Transportation costs had a greater impact on the profits of coffee since it had a smaller value per unit of volume. A simple calculation can show how this worked. If coffee had been exported via Izabal in 1853, transportation costs would have accounted for 24 percent of its price in London. In 1864, when the Panama route was in full service, transportation costs accounted for 14 percent of its price. That 10-percent difference, together with the savings in interest derived from a shorter trip, undoubtedly made the crop more attractive. A similar calculation for indigo, however, shows that, with the new trade routes, transportation costs for that product decreased from 6.9 to 3.2 percent of its London price. In the margin, coffee benefited more from the new transportation situation. . . .

Coffee did not become the main export overnight. Some of the reasons for this slow growth have been suggested above: resources were scarce and there was a limit to what the economy could accomplish. The shift to coffee production has to be viewed in the context of the alternatives available to the local producer. At appropriately outrageous interest rates it would have been possible to find capital to cover the country with coffee trees, but in order to do that all other activities would have had to come to a halt. Coffee was attractive up to a point, but there were other economic activities, such as indigo, food production, and commerce, that were also profitable. The entrepreneur, then, had to decide between a range of possibilities. When there was a product with a clear advantage, there were businessmen ready to seize the opportunity, as was the case with cotton in the 1860s.

The shift from indigo to coffee brought important changes to the economy. First, the economic geography of the country changed, the center of gravity moving from east to west. The eastern provinces of San Miguel and San Vicente produced almost 60 percent of all the indigo exported in 1858. The western and central provinces, in comparison, were best suited for the cultivation of coffee. The Lorenzo López census of 1858, which includes only the western provinces, shows that the efforts to cultivate the new crop were general throughout the region. In 1857 Santa Ana province had 439,980 trees in production and 1,400,630 planted but not ready yet to produce. Ahuachapán had 300,000 trees in production and 600,000 in nursery. Sonsonate had 67,865 trees already in production. Rich and poor, "both the landowner and the proletarian," were trying to produce coffee. . . .

None of the changes experienced by the Salvadoran economy during the second half of the century took place overnight. Events of great significance, like the opening of the Panama Railroad, gave clues to the economy, but the lack of resources slowed down growth. The importance of the opening of the Panama Railroad epitomizes two changes in the world economy that greatly affected El Salvador, but which were completely outside the sphere of influence of any Salvadoran individual or institution: (1) the transportation revolution and (2) the explosion of trade activity along the coast of the Pacific ocean. Conceivably this is a metaphor for one of the main characteristics of the modern Salvadoran economy, its helpless openness. When economists talk about the small-country hypothesis, countries unable to achieve any impact on international prices, the example of El Salvador comes to mind. . . .

There is no question about the importance of changes in the international markets, but this does not mean that the economic history of El Salvador is reduced to the study of those changes. The country had very specific characteristics that shaped its responses. First of all, it was a country where traditional agriculture had predominated for centuries and where few had the education necessary to function under the ever-changing environment of a very open economy demanding the learning of new agricultural technologies. Second, a government of indigo planters was delighted with the opportunity of expanding exports and did what it could to reinforce the trends. It subsidized the steamers of the Panama Railroad Company and improved the ports and the roads leading to them, encouraged coffee production, and rewarded it with land. Per-capita exports rose throughout the period but never reached the levels observed in other countries of Latin America. In 1880 Argentina, Uruguay, and Cuba, the most export-oriented countries in the region, "matched or exceeded the seventeen-dollar per-capita exports of the United States that year." El Salvador's per-capita exports that same year were around seven dollars. Even if the figure was relatively small, exports were the main source of income for a ruling elite that was eager for new sources of income.

Not So Liberal: Protectionist Peru

PAUL GOOTENBERG

Paul Gootenberg, author of *Between Silver and Guano: Commercial Policy and the State in Postindependence Peru* (1989), has long rejected the idea that unrestricted free-trade liberalism was imposed on early nineteenth-century Peru, or that it was easily accepted. Indeed, Gootenberg emphasizes the power of what he terms "protectionist elites" between 1820 and 1845, against whom only the landlord and merchant classes of southern Arequipa, whose fortunes had long been tied to exports of goods such as brandy, dissented. But the elites and popular classes of Lima were actively hostile to the notions of liberalized trade, preferring instead a more limited, controllable sphere for commerce and local industry. The severe political instability of the two decades following 1821 also made liberalized trade an unlikely stance. In part because of political turmoil, silver production had declined from its colonial levels, and paying for imports became difficult. As in Mexico, there was no particular enthusiasm for free trade, nor much incentive to pursue the policy.

By 1845, however, the growing export of guano (dried bird excrement) for use as a fertilizer in both Europe and the United States had apparently resolved the economic crisis of the immediate postindependence period. Unlike silver, whose production required substantial capital investment, guano could be collected almost costlessly. Guano exports grew very rapidly. Between 1842 and 1849, exports in metric tons grew nearly sevenfold. The profitability of the new trade underwrote the shift to trade liberalization. As Gootenberg puts it, "free trade became embodied in the larger fabric of national political stabilization" as elite merchants,

Paul Gootenberg, *Imagining Development. Economic Ideas in Peru's 'Fictitious Prosperity' of Guano, 1840–1880*, pp. 22–26, 33–35. Copyright © 1993 The Regents of the University of California. Reprinted by permission of the publisher.

Limeñan oligarchs, and the state jointly pursued the goals of profit, accumulation, consumption, and enhanced public revenues. By the same token, popular resistance to liberalized trade was submerged beneath the growing wave of imports that guano financed.

In other words, in Peru, the rise of free trade liberalism arrived not with Independence, but with the arrival of the guano boom and the stabilization of the liberal state. The enthusiasm for free trade—like earlier opposition to it—was essentially homegrown, and it depended as much on the vagaries of domestic economic and political circumstance as on the creation of a new international order by Great Britain. As Gootenberg writes in *Between Silver and Guano*, "liberalism required a modicum of economic and political stability to succeed."

From independence in 1821 to the mid 1840s, the Peruvian "republic" slogged through decades of unrelenting caudillo strife and bewildering political and regional disintegrations. Colonial economic foundations collapsed as haciendas, mines, workshops, and trading towns slumped into abandon and disrepair. Plagued by some twenty-four major regime changes in as many years (and countless smaller *golpes* and wider regional wars), Peru's anarchy was enough to blur all initial visions of nationhood. Only the age of guano rescued Peru from its catastrophic age of caudillos—elevating the economic liberalism of the stable export state into a veritable act of national salvation. Yet the new Peru remained awash in the wakes, however muddled, of two prior (even colonial) currents of national economic thought. Along with its caudillo skirmishes, postindependence Peru had just ended a bitter, three-decade battle over protectionism and free trade as the country struggled to define itself in the emerging global order.

Conservative Peru was not then a country born liberal. Volatile but largely forgotten economic-nationalist ideologies, interests, movements, and policies permeated its earliest regimes and first yearnings for development. One strain was eminently elitist, the other profoundly popular, but together they smothered Peru's feeble first generation of theoretical free-traders. Of import here is the influence such crude national ideologies would exert on later developmentalist thinkers of the export era, even after being roundly defeated and disgraced in the late 1840s. Unlike purist Peruvian liberals—who could draw on a vast body of formal European theory—Peruvian dissenters had to piece together their own reflections and critiques out of hard economic experience and local ideas. . . .

A Protection of Elites

The protectionism of elites from 1820 to 1845 was in part a carry-over of colonial corporate mentalities and partly a new defensive action wrapped after 1821 in the symbols of Western nationalism. All sectors of the Peruvian upper classes shared in this movement: the Lima commercial *consulado* (merchant guild), shippers, coastal sugar planters, urban millers, finance cliques, provincial traders, landlords, and textile makers, as well as nationalist officers, diplomats, and politicians. Their center of gravity, however, would remain the traditional geopolitical one of viceregal Lima. Stiff tariffs, import prohibitions, exclusions of foreign traders, discriminatory trade treaties, and national monopolies and privileges were among their primitive, homegrown practices. Spokesmen justified such policies out of sheer nativism, the need to promote a "national capitalist class" for an infirm state, compensatory advantages for beleaguered hijo del país entrepreneurs, a complementary "economic independence," integration of far-flung economic sectors, correction of trade imbalances, the conservation of employment and skills, and time-honored notions of social harmony. There was also the historical example set by the mercantilist rise of Britain and France into great trader and industrial nations—that is, before they began preaching free trade to Peru.

Because Peru's nationalist groundswell came by and large as a defensive move against both the novel competition of North Atlantic trades in the region and the first inklings of liberal trade theory, it was not especially coherent or versed in the tenets of emergent classical theory. In streams of pamphlets, petitions, and polemics to generals and ministers, aroused writers drew on glorified notions of self-interest (elevated into reasons of state), espoused mercantilist or physiocratic principles (including a waning bullionism), or mimicked the autarkic mentalities of the archaic Hapsburg colonial state. Sometimes they recited a litany of obscure, eighteenth-century Spanish "economists"—including the ever popular Jovellanos—and remained steadfast admirers of Colbertian achievements or of Argüelles's more contemporary Spanish industrial variant. Even deep in the Andean interior, economic thinking spread, reflected in passionate *Cuzqueño* protectionist pleas or, for a curious example, in a remote Ayacuchan translation of a French text on political economy—annotated with rejoinders to the inapplicable free-trade doctrines of the author (P. H. Suzanne). Lima, as a political port city, enjoyed elaborate cosmopolitan traditions, in intellectual life at least, and literate Limeños devoured in their feisty and varied press a rich menu of economic histories, overseas policy studies, and, with some lag, the latest in European political economy. Yet the newfangled open trade theories of Bastiat, Say, and Smith—voiced by a handful of timid Peruvian liberals and crusading foreign consuls—were routinely dismissed by nationalist spokesmen as "inappropriate," "slavish," "ruinous," "self-interested," "hypocritical," and "unrealistic" for Peru.

Such nationalist negations did not quite add up to a working formula for development, though they often revealed astute criticisms of commercial growth and an unmistakable sense of national self-interest. Nor were Peruvian elites alone, for similar concoctions of nationalist passions and interests swept early economic debates in sister republics such as Mexico, Argentina, and Colombia. But above all they faithfully reflected the crushing economic contractions of the postindependence years and elite anxieties of displacement by interloping foreigners.

Actions spoke louder than words—and to a large degree, interest lapsed in all grand schemes as statesmen coped with the quotidian traumas of meeting imaginary budgets and paying for real wars. Throughout the era the few hundred surviving top national merchants patently resisted openings to freer trade and the material lures of the two dozen or so liberal foreign houses in their midst. Constraints of every sort fell on the port's overseas shippers and retailers. The contrast could not be sharper with the eagerly internationalist Peruvian merchants of the guano age. The organized consulado's timely fiscal and administrative aid to Lima's ephemeral state allowed officials and militarists to deflect incessant foreign free-trade pressures against Peru's web of commercial restrictions and navigation acts. Sugar planters, a faltering but critical commercial force all along the northern coast, championed a sheltered bilateral trade system with Chile, in lieu of still imaginary outlets to the Atlantic. In this long campaign a host of related coastal farmers joined forces against invading foodstuffs: foreign flour, tobacco, rice, lard, wine. These early defenders of regional markets contrast with the agrarian export oligarchy that would dominate Peruvian agriculture by the later half of the guano age.

Andean traders and *hacendados* were mainly out to sustain time-honored interior trade routes or to protect their *obrajes*, the scattered colonial-style wool and cotton manufactories of the highlands. Provincials proved remarkably adept in 1820s political bids to stem the flood of industrial textiles from Britain and the United States, at times weaving complex arguments for the factory cause. To sympathetic congresses, spokesmen wrapped their concern in Peru's burning desire for national "industry," though the inefficient and primitive obrajes were a dying breed. Guano-age politicians became anything but industrial sympathizers. A veritable horde of *Gamarrista* military chiefs (followers of the central conservative figure, Mariscal Agustín Gamarra) sized up pressures from merchants and rural artisans and launched volatile antiforeign crusades that paralyzed overseas initiatives and investments. Even Cerro de Pasco silver miners, the era's one recuperating export group, rejected offers to open mining to foreign capital and expertise (fearing ownership loss) and joined with influential Limeño merchants instead for state-sponsored mine projects. . . .

Guild protectionism, too, was eminently defensive. Artisans sought to shelter, through high tariffs and outright prohibitions, their light craft manufactures. Their prime concern lay in promotion of skilled labor and employment, not in improved technology, efficiency, scale, or industrialism (Lima still had no factories to speak of). At the same time, to many, artisans colorfully and convincingly wrapped their aims in the national interest, epitomizing the flesh-and-blood hijos del país. To the guilds, foreign merchants and crafts—such as the novel, mass-produced, up-market imports that flooded Lima in the late 1820s—were unnecessary, ruinous, unfair, and downright unpatriotic. Such competition was forcing Peru's long-suffering model citizens into lives of vagrancy, vice, and political mayhem—a most frequent and threatening motif. Craft leaders invoked the standard of the "honorable," "humble," and "democratic" artisan. They vaunted republicanism and popular education. Their earnest work ethic and simple skills were assets to the nation, and their political and fiscal health a prop to republicanism, which obviously had to heed the needs of "the people." Vague notions of a fixed "just price" infused this quasi-market mentality, immediately turned against new external competitors, too. Autodidactic craft leaders could also list their favorite Spanish economists, but mostly they railed against "imitative systems," "theories applied to other countries"—but just not right for conditions in Peru. As in elite discourse, countless special "exceptions" took precedence over the finer dictates of free trade. Hardly radicals—their very existence hinged on upper-class patrons—artisans profusely apologized for their "affronts to the lights of the century." Still, they boldly warned that if Peru lost its sparse indigenous skills, it would become "tributary of whoever approaches our shores to trade."

If virtually an instinctual mode of thinking, craft political economy closely resembled that of better-read Continental artisans, who occasionally enriched their ranks, and of counterparts in every Latin American town with colonial guild survivals—Bogotá, Santiago, Puebla. Besides stiff craft tariffs, popular welfare would also be advanced by lower-cost mass necessities (for instance, imported foodstuffs, tools, and typical manufacturing inputs such as foreign cloth). Peru's responsive tariff structure thus provided artisans with the advantages of what is now termed effective protection. It was the state's "duty" to support native "industry," as aptly expressed in frequent military supply contracts for fancy uniforms and the like. Because craftsmanship centered on quality items for a remnant colonial aristocracy, artisans continued to be obsessed with taste considerations rather than cost. They boasted the superior quality of home goods over flimsy, cut-rate imports. Hierarchic guild masters tried, without much success, to carry on as well with restrictive guild statutes, which supposedly regulated quality, training, and entry, but they warmly welcomed the trickle of new European craft immigrants to Lima. "Teachers" and "models," their tasteful creations and techniques would spill over to ill-trained native artisans and shopkeepers.

As a protectionism, artisan political economy proved absolute, since labor efficiency and final cost were hardly its central concerns. To portray such popular philosophy as a consistent, much less viable, conception of "development" would be an exaggeration. Much like elite nationalism, it basically thrived on hard times.

Still, this amalgam of petit bourgeois notions proved highly workable in early republican politics. Peddling their ideas with timely petitions and protests, Lima guilds had won tariffs of 50 to 90 percent by the late 1820s, followed by a host of full import prohibitions during Peru's "prohibitions era" of 1828–1840. In their campaigns guild leaders could exploit their business and political connections to elite merchants and suppliers. Other aspects of their program found their way into policy (such as pro-artisan immigration law), and even after textile and other tariffs fell by the wayside in the 1840s, urban crafts remained under special protective duties. Throughout the era their impassioned pleas rang in the Lima press and eloquent memorials (such as that of the cigar maker José María García before the full 1849 congress). Guilds cut deals with caudillos, candidates, and political clubs and packed the chambers to cheer or jeer congressional delegates. What artisan appeal lacked in economic theory, or sense, it made up by embodying heartfelt desires for national dignity and popular progress.

PART III

Trade, Finance, and Industrialization, 1870–1930

The mature export economies that appeared in Latin America after 1850 were the product of circumstances that raised the profitability and volume of international trade. Between the 1820s and the 1870s, for example, transatlantic freight rates fell sharply, to little more than half what they had been in 1820. The reduction in transportation costs permitted traders to profit from progressively smaller differences in prices and to enlarge the volume of trade. At the same time, the terms of trade, or prices of Latin American exports relative to imports, also improved. Brazil's terms of trade, for example, increased substantially between the 1820s and the 1850s. The improvement in the Mexican terms of trade was less pronounced, but Mexico's terms of trade were still nearly 50 percent higher in the 1880s than they had been sixty years earlier. Thus the purchasing power of exports grew as the cost of transporting them fell. In other words, the potential profits from trade increased.

At the same time, growing political stability in countries such as Argentina and Mexico made both trade and investment less risky. Foreign merchants and investors, who had previously seen themselves as targets of impoverished regimes, were now courted. Some countries—Mexico was one—organized expositions and trade fairs to reassure foreign businessmen and to spread the news that Latin America was "open for business." Flattering portraits of national leaders appeared in the foreign press, and prospectuses for investment schemes promised high profits. The operation of the gold standard, which flourished between 1870 and 1914, facilitated the transfer of savings from lender to borrower by providing broadly predictable exchange rates, making calculations of foreign profits in home currencies easier. As a result, international lending to Latin America resumed by the 1860s, with Argentina, Brazil, Chile, and Peru as its prime beneficiaries. There were further interruptions in the 1870s, and with the Baring Crisis in the 1890s, but Argentina, Brazil, and Mexico generally attracted considerable direct investment. Foreign bondholders lent to Argentina and Uruguay as well.

Underlying these developments was a profound change in the structure of the world economy. The industrialization of Great Britain and continental Europe raised the European demand for foodstuffs, fibers, and raw materials. At the same time, the products of industrialization were now available for international consumption. Latin America was by no means an insignificant market, even though D. C. M. Platt suggested as much, particularly before 1860, in *Latin America and British Trade, 1806–1914* (1972). For example, according to D. A. Farnie, *The English Cotton Industry and the World Market, 1815–1896* (1979), Latin America (including the West Indies) bought 21 percent of the volume of British exports of cotton piece goods in 1820. Latin America's share peaked in 1840 at about 32 percent. By 1850, it had fallen to some 24 percent, but this was still no less than India's share of about 23 percent. As late as 1903, Brazil was still the largest single market for Lancashire cottons, and after the 1870s, Argentina's participation in the trade grew quickly.

The expansion of exports from Latin America financed increased imports. Victor Bulmer-Thomas calculates that for Latin America as a whole, the annual rate of growth of exports between 1850 and around 1912 was 3.9 percent. Yet there was considerable difference in performance throughout the region. Argentina's record, at 6.1 percent per year, was exceptional, while the performance of Haiti (1.5 percent) or Honduras (1.4 percent) was dismal. If the yardstick of comparison is the median rate of growth (3.4 percent)—the rate dividing the spread of observations in half—then Argentina, Brazil, Colombia (including Panama), Costa Rica, the Dominican Republic, Ecuador, Guatemala, and Paraguay all did better than average. Poorer performers included Cuba and Puerto Rico, which is surprising, and Mexico, which is less so. Even in the heyday of open economies, a "typical" rate of export growth is difficult to determine. Argentina and Chile, which seemed on the verge of attaining developed status in 1870, fell behind when viewed from the perspective of the developed countries a century later. A sustained expansion of the Mexican economy did not really occur until the middle of the 1890s and was ultimately cut short by financial crisis and revolution. There were, in short, a variety of export experiences in the later nineteenth century.

The articles that follow consider some of the questions that have intrigued scholars. Roberto Cortés Conde provides an overview of export-led growth in Latin America. Albert Fishlow analyzes the way international capital markets functioned and explains why and how problems of payment sometimes occurred. Alec Ford asks whether the gold standard made a difference, and if it helped stabilize the Latin American economies. Alan Taylor focuses on the connection between immigration, savings, and economic growth in Argentina. And Stephen Haber shows how the interruption of international trade during the Great Depression affected Brazilian industrialization.

Export-Led Growth in Latin America

ROBERTO CORTÉS CONDE

Roberto Cortés Conde is author or editor of numerous books, including *The First Stages of Modernization of Spanish America* (1974) and *Dinero, dueda y crisis: evolución fiscal y monetaria en la Argentina, 1862–1890* (1989). The article reprinted here looks primarily at Argentina, Brazil, and Mexico in the latter half of the nineteenth century and attempts to draw some tentative generalizations. Cortés Conde presents a balanced view of the impact of export growth on these economies. One the one hand, he rejects what he terms the "extreme, oversimplified view that [export-led] growth did not produce any benefit for the domestic economy," a view he associates more with what he terms "neomarxian" writers such as André Gunder Frank than with dependency writing per se.

Roberto Cortés Conde, "Export-Led Growth in Latin America, 1870–1930," *Journal of Latin American Studies,* 24: Quincentenary Supplement (1992), pp. 163–168, 178–179. Reprinted by permission of Cambridge University Press.

But on the other hand, he emphasizes that specialization in commodity production usually meant that export earnings were very unstable, since the prices at which wheat, beef, coffee, sugar and other goods sold were volatile and usually beyond the control of the producer nation.

It is worth emphasizing just how rapidly production grew in some cases. In his *Essays on the Economic History of the Argentine Republic* (1970) Carlos Díaz Alejandro estimated that real per capita Argentine GDP grew at at least 1.6 percent per year in the fifty years preceding World War I. Markos Mamalakis (*The Growth and Structure of the Chilean Economy: From Independence to Allende,* 1976) guesses that per capita income in Chile grew at 2 percent per year between 1850 and 1930, meaning that it doubled every 35 years. This rate of growth is very substantial. In both countries, greater participation in the world economy corresponded to increased, not diminished rates of growth, as dependency models might suggest. By contrast, Nathaniel Leff estimates that per capita income growth in nineteenth-century Brazil was slow, although total income growth probably exceeded 1.8 percent per year in *Underdevelopment and Development in Brazil* (1982). A recent survey of Mexican income growth in the early nineteenth century concludes that national income could have grown at no more than 1 percent a year in the first half of the nineteenth century. Between 1860 and 1910, according to John Coatsworth's estimates in his "Obstacles to Economic Development in Nineteenth-Century Mexico," *American Historical Review* (1978), this rate may have reached 3 percent per year or even more. Latin American economies, in other words, varied considerably; at least in Argentina and Mexico, growth accelerated dramatically in the second half of the nineteenth century and the volume of exports grew substantially. As Cortés Conde makes clear, these positive experiences shaped Latin American thinking down through the 1920s. "Export pessimism" came later, and it received substantial reinforcement from the collapse of international trade during the Great Depression.

In 1949 Raúl Prebisch, an Argentine economist, published a study for the United Nations' Economic Commission for Latin America (ECLA), in which he attributed the failure to reach sustained economic growth in Latin America to the international division of labour. Based on research carried out by ECLA on the terms of trade between manufactures and primary goods, he concluded that—contrary to expectations—they moved against primary products. If prices decline as productivity increases (in competitive markets), industrial goods, where the technological improvements had been more significant, should have declined in price more than agricultural goods. The empirical results of the study showed the opposite. If the Latin American countries therefore wanted to benefit from technological progress, they should move towards industrialisation. Almost at the same time, based on the same empirical study, Hans Singer not only argued that the gains from trade had not been distributed equally, but also that foreign investments in the export sector were not part of the domestic economy, but represented an enclave belonging to the countries of the centre which received its benefits. Singer advanced an argument that became popular later on; he noted the existence in the underdeveloped countries of a dual economy with two sectors each with different productivity and segmented markets: a modern sector linked to the central countries and a traditional sector linked to the rest of the economy. Also, from the critics of the classical theory of trade, another argument was put forward: the different income elasticities of demand for manufactures and agricultural goods (Engels' law) suggested that expenditure on agricultural goods would decline in relative terms as incomes rose, hurting the terms of trade for primary products. All these arguments led to the conclusion that Latin American countries could not expect very much from the future evolution of international trade. Instead, they had to look to their own domestic markets. Industrialisation oriented to the internal protected market was the obvious way. This was, however, very different from the view contemporaries held at the beginning of this century.

There was impressive growth in some Latin American countries before the First World War. Chile, Mexico, Argentina and Brazil seemed to have left behind decades of anarchy and economic backwardness to begin a process of remarkable growth. The exploitation of untapped natural resources, which those countries had in abundance, had produced a sudden and impressive increase in their wealth. Lacking domestic or neighbouring markets (due to the same backwardness), the exploitation of those resources was conditioned by the lowering of maritime freight rates from their very high levels in the mid-nineteenth century. The dramatic decline of ocean freight rates in the second half of the century (especially for bulky goods) allowed the products of the Western hemisphere to reach North Atlantic markets. The same decline of freight rates and a favourable institutional framework allowed the free movement not only of goods, but also of capital and labour.

The new countries of the Western hemisphere, despite their wealth of resources, lacked capital (especially to build land transportation networks) and labour. Those countries found a market for goods and a supply of factors (capital and labour) in the old continent. To a large extent, part of the capital was forward savings on future export earnings that assumed the form of huge debts to be paid later on with the increased income left by the rise of trade. In this way, Mexico, Brazil and Argentina built their railway systems, allowing them to end economic isolation of the fragmented and narrow markets (see table).

Although contemporaries considered the advantage of exploiting abundant natural resources to be self-evident, it was also true that the whole process was not always smooth. The exploitation of natural resources produced a sudden increase of wealth. After a certain point, it produced a climate of bonanza which attracted more capital and labour. When capital and labour began to yield diminishing returns (or natural resources were exhausted) or demand had changed, the boom was followed by a bust.

When the expansion was halted, everybody questioned what had happened with the income created during the boom. To what extent had it been saved or contributed to the formation of capital? Had it been totally dissipated in luxury consumption or remitted abroad by foreign factors of production?

These economies suffered from wide fluctuations which the producers did not control. These fluctuations were linked to supply (availability and return of natural resources) and changing condi-

Exports of Mexico, Chile and Argentina, 1870–1900

Year	Mexico 1900=100	Chile $ gold m.	Argentina $ gold m.
1870	NA	68.4	30
1877	51.2	69.4	45
1887	65.9	125.7	84
1900	100.0	167.7	155

tions in international markets (sugar, nitrates). Moreover, while the markets fluctuated sharply in price, supply for technical reasons required longer periods for adjustment (e.g. coffee and cattle-raising).

It is also necessary to remember that the 1870–95 period was one of declining international prices (particularly for agricultural goods). This was due to a large extent to supply at lower prices from countries of recent settlement. The effect of declining prices was offset by the higher returns from new lands, but this put strong pressure on the need for efficiency gains which in some periods severely hurt marginal producers in the new countries.

At the beginning of the twentieth century there were rising prices in international markets which brought an impressive rate of capital accumulation in some of those countries and at the same time produced an overexpansion (marginal lands at lower prices were intramarginal at higher ones). This had negative effects when it was necessary to adjust supply to changing prices. The extensive growth continued until the eve of World War I. The Balkan crisis was a warning, but then conditions during war years demanded large supplies of certain commodities (e.g. military raw materials such as copper, nitrates and food) which maintained production at high levels. The end of the war created additional demand that led to an unprecedented increase in supply. Once reconstruction was under way, market conditions began to change and the European supply of goods and the replacement of some products (sugar beet instead of sugar cane, artificial nitrates instead of natural ones) negatively affected markets for primary products. Chile, Cuba, Brazil and Argentina in the 1920s suffered a crisis as a result of these changes.

It was not only the problematic adjustment to new market conditions after the troublesome war years that led to a new equilibrium. There were also changes in policies in favour of autarky that produced long-standing consequences. The autarkic policies followed by European countries and the United States, under the pretext of securing supplies of basic goods in case of war, ended an era in which markets were relatively free and competitive. For a decade it was thought that this was just a short-term problem and that normal market conditions would soon be restored. Furthermore, the commercial problems of the 1920s were eased by the rise in international capital flows (with U.S. capital in particular replacing British sources of funds).

The 1930s crisis and the depression that followed sustained these pessimistic views. The fall of income and employment in the industrialised countries was reflected in a fall in their demand for primary products and a catastrophic fall in prices and world trade. Even when the economic recovery of trade (e.g. wheat, coffee) was sooner than expected, the long duration of the depression confirmed the idea that the 'belle époque' of world trade had finished and every country had to follow the protectionist policies of the big powers looking to their domestic markets as the main determinant of aggregate demand. Keynes provided theoretical grounds for this belief with his argument that there was structural disequilibrium in the labour market which was extended to the theory of international trade.

For those who wrote in the first years after the Second World War, the experience of the 1920s and 1930s was so close that it encouraged pessimistic theories of trade, far away from the mainstream of economics (e.g. Prebisch). Their concerns over trends in world trade were accompanied by a serious preoccupation with the possibilities of massive unemployment in the postwar years, once the conditions of the belligerent nations had been normalised and they reinitiated their manufactured exports to Latin America. Based on that interpretation they recommended policies leading to the promotion, through strong protectionist measures and subsidies, of a process of industrialisation oriented to the internal market. Their interpretation was strongly biased by the need to find historical examples to defend those policies. Searching for favourable arguments, they turned to the schemes provided by the German historical school at the end of the nineteenth century. The German historical school had also been influential in some South American countries. In Chile and Argentina Francisco Encina and Alejandro Bunge, an historian and economist respectively, who had both strongly influenced Aníbal Pinto and Raúl Prebisch, had started their professional careers in an intellectual climate dominated by Friedrich List. Singer and Furtado recently acknowledged the same influence, which was also recognised in the case of W. W. Rostow.

Supported by the authority of such authors, protectionist policies were recommended to help 'infant industries' and to maintain the level of employment. These writers also defended active intervention by the state in the economy to reorient local savings to the protected sector. It was believed that good rulers advised by wise economists equipped with the latest macroeconomic tools, would overcome market failures to avoid repeating past mistakes (based on excessive confidence in market forces and international trade), thus guaranteeing a process of autonomous self-sustained growth. Yet what were the characteristics of export-led growth which made such growth ephemeral? What was the main characteristic of those economies in the late nineteenth century and what was the effect that the rise in exports had on the economy as a whole?

The distinctive feature of these economies from the demand-side was the lack of domestic or neighbouring markets for the production of goods based on natural resources. This was the reason for their dependence on foreign markets. On the supply-side there was an abundance of natural resources, but an almost total lack of capital and—in some cases—even of labour. The fall in ocean freights allowed the products of those countries to reach North Atlantic markets and at the same time permitted the inflow of capital and labour from the countries where those markets were located.

The markets for goods as well as the markets for factors were in foreign countries. To what extent, therefore, was the control of demand and the remittance of profits and wages in the hands of foreign interests? The extreme case was that of an enclave, in which there was no increase in domestic demand, nor an increase in saving that could contribute to capital accumulation. Other explanations focused on the distortions that led to monoculture (higher returns in the agricultural sector attracted investments and made the structure of supply simpler whereas increasing income widened the demand, Furtado). Some others emphasised the vulnerability to external fluctuations (Ferrer, Pinto) and the impossibility of carrying out compensatory anticyclical policies when aggregate demand was mainly determined by foreign factors (Ferrer).

A new school, the 'dependentistas', subsequently made a slight change in the basic argument of the literature on economic development of the 1950s and 1960s. They accepted the importance of export earnings for the formation of national markets and capital accumulation in the developing (periphery) countries, but they noted that the level of capital accumulation was dependent upon foreign demand and the level of capital accumulation in advanced (centre) countries. The neomarxians, on the other hand, argued that the lack of capital accumulation in the periphery was a necessary result of the capital accumulation in the centre which extracted a surplus from the primary-producing countries. Underdevelopment in the Third World was a counterpart of the development of the First World (Gunder Frank).

From the other side, even in the 1950s there were strong warnings against interpretations and recommendations that might lead to inward-looking policies with a strong anti-export bias. Haberler formulated a serious criticism of the terms of trade argument, insisting that there existed just one standard economy theory stressing the benefits of international trade. There also appeared in the 1960s two books which from different perspectives rebutted the basic conceptions of the critics of trade. One was by Carlos Díaz-Alejandro on Argentina. The other was by Warren Dean, discussing Furtado's main argument on the effect of coffee exports on the Brazilian economy. Further on, different studies, to some extent following the interpretation of the staple theory for Canada and the United States (Innis, Wilkins), argued that in certain cases export had a positive effect on the rest of the economy. . . .

A review of the literature on these different national cases does not allow us to reach definitive conclusions on the advantages or disadvantages of the Latin American experience of growth through trade. The extreme, oversimplified idea that this growth did not produce any benefit for the domestic economy, but only for the metropolitan countries with which it traded, nowadays seems totally discredited. Moreover, the authors mentioned underline some positive effects: the widening of the market, the construction of the infrastructure of production and the imports of capital goods for new domestic industries. On the other hand, it is impossible to disregard some serious problems associated with export-led growth, e.g. wide fluctuations in price resulting from changing patterns of demand or supply. Even more important, resources began to decline or were affected by diminishing returns. How to replace those resources and adjust the economy to the changing conditions of supply when the early favourable relation between resources and population had been modified were some of the most urgent problems.

Even though those problems were not overcome, it now seems that the alternatives chosen—inward-oriented growth, protectionism with total disregard for the availability of resources—have not been any more successful solutions for these economies.

Lessons from the Past

ALBERT FISHLOW

Albert Fishlow has written a number of influential publications, including *American Railroads and the Transformation of the Antebellum Economy* (1965), "Lessons from the 1890s for the 1980s," in Guillermo Calvo et al., *Debt Stabilization and Development: Essays in Memory of Carlos Díaz Alejandro* (1989), and "Origins and Consequences of Import Substitution in Brazil," in Luis di Marco, ed., *International Trade and Economic Development: Essays in Honor of Raul Prebisch* (1982). In the paper excerpted here, Fishlow stresses the importance of foreign borrowing in the economies of Argentina and Brazil, among other nations in Latin America. Fishlow suggests that the patterns of borrowing and lending explain the ease or difficulty with which countries could repay their debts. He emphasizes a number of crucial factors, including whether countries borrowed to finance investment or simply to compensate for an inability to raise revenues by taxation. If borrowing led to investment in productive assets, income growth could help repay borrowings, even if the timetable of loan payments did not always coincide exactly with the growth in earnings from exports. Since a growth in export earnings made it possible to repay past borrowings, the level of export prices and the willingness of other nations to purchase exports affected the financial condition of the borrowers. The Baring Crisis of 1890 is an example of what Fishlow terms a "developmental default," a crisis in which the debtor was temporarily unable to generate sufficient income to service its debts, but was by no means without the assets necessary to repay them.

However, if a country borrowed to finance consumption, it could expect no future growth in income to make repayment easier. Although Fishlow pays particular attention to the Peruvian case, many examples could be cited of this kind of largely unproductive borrowing. For instance, in 1827, Mexico defaulted on bonds it had issued on the London market in 1824 and 1825 (in what Fishlow terms a "public revenue default") precisely because the proceeds of the loans were used to pay both for unusual mili-

Albert Fishlow, "Lessons from the Past: Capital Markets During the Nineteenth Century and the Interwar Period," *International Organization,* 39:3 (1985), 383–386, 392–393, 399–401, 402–405. Reprinted by permission of the MIT Press Journals and the author.

tary expenditures and for the costs of public administration. Fishlow's attribution of public sector insolvency to "stagnating economies whose governments financed current outlays with loans that they were able to get by paying exorbitantly high interest rates" captures well Mexican conditions in the early nineteenth century. Despite repeated attempts to reach settlement with the foreign bondholders (in 1831, 1837, 1846, and 1850), the Mexican foreign debt remained in default until 1887. The penalty for such a default could be quite high. For Mexico, the threat of national bankruptcy was a nearly permanent feature during the nineteenth century.

In short, Fishlow's useful distinctions remind us that "debt crises" in Latin America were by no means all the same.

On Friday, 13 August 1982, Finance Minster Jesús Silva Herzog of Mexico made a series of visits to the International Monetary Fund, the Federal Reserve, and the U.S. Treasury. His message to each was the same: Mexico could no longer continue to service its debt. Thus began a dramatic weekend of negotiations that marked the end of the preceding decade's buoyant expansion of developing country debt and the start of a still continuing response to the sudden collapse.

Joseph Kraft describes the Mexican action as "a bombshell that shook an entire universe. It was like Columbus setting out on an uncharted sea, and taking with him on the leap into the dark some of the stuffiest people in some of the world's most hidebound institutions." Kraft, like many others, is too much struck by the novelty of the event. More than a century earlier, in a paper read to the Statistical Society in London, Hyde Clarke had lamented the "unparalleled disaster . . . which has inflicted not only pecuniary, but moral and even physical distress, on every family of Western Europe which had the industry to secure and the thrift to save." One could go back even farther than the crisis of the 1870s to find similar reactions attending the defaults of the 1820s, in which Latin America, and Mexico, played a principal part.

International capital markets functioned, and failed, long before this latest episode. And they played even more central roles than in recent years. From 1870 to 1914, for example, a truly global economy was forged for the first time, extending from the core of Western European industrializers to latecomers in Eastern Europe to raw material suppliers on the periphery. At the heart of this extension of trade was a system of expanding finance that girded the globe with railways and opened new areas for primary production. Large infusions of capital provided the savings, and the foreign exchange to import track and equipment, that were beyond the capacities of recipient countries. The amounts were enormous: in the four decades before the First World War something like $30 billion, the equivalent in 1984 dollars of $270 billion or one-third of contemporary developing country debt, in a world economy perhaps one-tenth as large.

For the suppliers of capital, such flows meant large allocations from their own savings. Britain, the largest source of foreign capital, invested abroad an annual average of 5 percent of gross product during the period 1873–1913, reaching a peak of 10 percent just before the outbreak of war. For France, the commitment was about half as large, both on average and also for the final surge in 1910–13. Germany was a latecomer. Its more rapid growth and absorption of saving in domestic capital formation left a small 2 percent of income for overseas assets, and a lesser tendency for acceleration. The contrast to the recent expansion of lending to developing countries is marked: even during the peak transfers of the 1970s only about 1 percent of industrialized countries' incomes was being channeled in that direction.

Foreign investment was central to the trade and growth performance of most of the recipients in the late 19th century. Australia, Canada, Argentina, and Brazil all experienced surges of capital imports that accounted for a third to a half of all domestic investment undertaken. The United States, despite its position as the largest capital importer in the 19th-century world economy, was an exception. Foreign lending accounted for no more than 10 to 15 percent of investment, and that only for selected peak years. That lower level is much more the standard of recent years. During the most buoyant phase of increasing debt in the last decade foreign saving financed about 20 percent of developing country investment, higher only for the low-income and poorly performing African countries.

The First World War marked a decisive break. For one, it marked the emergence of the United States for the first time as a net creditor nation. For another, the position of the principal European lenders was much changed. Germany became a leading importer of capital; French assets abroad were dramatically reduced by the repudiation of extensive Russian holdings, diminishing the appetite for overseas holdings as domestic reconstruction requirements increased; Britain experienced a marked decline in savings rates. A larger U.S. presence did not compensate for European withdrawal, and global foreign investment declined.

In addition, developmental finance for the periphery took second place during the 1920s to capital flows among the industrialized countries and lending for war reconstruction. Reparations and the interally loans were a constant source of irritation. Then came the Great Depression, the demise of the gold standard, and widespread default. The level of world trade rapidly declined after 1929, and interdependence produced perverse consequences for peripheral participants. This post-1914 failure of the international capital market was in stark contrast to pre-1914 success. No wonder, then, the nostalgia for 19th-century conditions that W. A. Lewis reflected in the introduction to his survey of the interwar period: "The sixty years before 1914 witnessed an astonishing expansion of the world economy, in area, in production, in interdependence, and in complexity. Why did progress reduce, not indeed to a halt, but to a much slower pace after 1918?"

The subject of international capital flows over more than three-quarters of a century is a vast one. Several works, some classics, have been dedicated to the topic. My objective here is not to retell the vivid and fascinating story nor even to rehearse earlier debates of the causes and the consequences of foreign investment. I seek rather to distill some of its important features for comparison with the present. For the pre-1914 period, the central issues are why the market worked so well and how it managed the periodic fluctuations in economic activity that afflicted borrowers and lenders alike. For the interwar period, parallel questions relate to the breakdown of the earlier model.

I shall stress four determinants of capital market performance. The first is the principal use that borrowing countries made of international finance. Recipients could use the resources to supplement their own domestic savings and increase investment or to enhance consumption. In practice, before 1914 and to some extent even before 1929, this was a decision to invest in infrastructure or to finance current governmental expenditures. The former almost always translated into greater capital formation, the latter into consumption outlays. Note that the distinction is *not* between private and public borrowing. Governments could and did apply resources to state-owned projects; but then they would have to find the means to service their debts. Not all had and have the political capacity to do so.

A second important factor is the ease with which debtor countries increase exports. Foreign capital inflows imposed the requirement of subsequent outflows to service interest and profits, as well as amortization. There was a question not only of whether borrowed resources would earn an adequate rate of return but also of how to transfer those earnings. The answer depends, in the last analysis, upon export capacity and the structure of world trade.

The third characteristic I single out is the institutional form of financial intermediation. Results are not independent of the way that funds are channeled, whether through the large investment banks centered in London before 1914, banks in the United States in the interwar period, or the Euromarket in the 1970s and 1980s. Very obviously, the International Monetary Fund is a central and new actor on the scene, but private agents and national governments performed at least some of its functions earlier.

Finally, the source of finance shaped the quantities and consequences of capital flows. The degree of politicization and the consequent direction of foreign investment differed with its national origin. London, Paris, Berlin and New York were not perfect substitutes, and capital markets were not and are not fully blind to the identity of transactors. There is also a second indirect route of influence via international trade. The ability of borrowers to apply their proceeds freely, and to find markets for their exports to service their foreign obligations, varies with the policies and practices of creditor countries.

Together, these four characteristics add up to distinctive equilibrating mechanisms of trade, capital movements, service payments, and income of the global economy, both historically and at the present time. Such relationships embody an important political component, as noted above, but also a dominant economic content. The appeal of the profit motive, and the private returns that could be earned, mobilized capital. The search for profit did not mean a perfect capital market, but it did mean a market and an international economy within which it functioned. . . .

Developmental Finance

Developmental investment of the first, market-oriented kind was largely directed to railroads and other infrastructure. Railroads alone represented more than 40 percent of British asset holdings in 1913. (With full allowance for the direct governmental loans also applied for this purpose, one contemporary placed the total at 60 percent). Matthew Simon's breakdown of all borrowing between 1865 and 1914 by economic sector allocates 69 percent to social overhead capital, with extractive industry in second place, far behind at 12 percent. By contrast, holdings of foreign governments outside the Empire made up less than 10 percent of the portfolio in 1913. Not only had foreign holdings fallen from almost one-half of British investment in 1870, there was even a decline in absolute terms.

These data derive from securities that were publicly issued. Of them, about four-fifths in 1913 were debentures and one-fifth was in the form of equity participation. Direct investment in enterprises and activities not represented by issues traded on the Stock Exchange might have accounted for something like 10 percent of total British investment at the time of the war.

The intent underlying all this investment was well understood. Sir George Paish could take satisfaction in 1909 at the role capital exports had played in contributing to British trade and prosperity: "By building railways for the world, and especially the young countries, we have enabled the world to increase its production of wealth at a rate never previously witnessed and to produce those things which this country is especially desirous of purchasing—foodstuffs and raw materials. Moreover, by assisting other countries to increase their output of the commodities they were specially fitted to produce, our investors have helped those countries to secure the means of purchasing the goods that Great Britain manufactures." Credit advanced in the first stage would lead to the purchase of British capital goods. In the second stage a return flow of peripheral primary exports would cover the requisite payments of interest and dividends, lowering the cost of living at the center as well.

Flows of capital from Britain thus went where real returns were likely to be greatest, that is, where new lands to be exploited were receiving labor through immigration. Large waves of emigration from overcrowded Europe moved in conjunction with financial credits. Foreign investment went not to the poorest countries but to the richest, those where incomes even exceeded those of the capital-supplying countries. The tropical countries, already burdened with high population densities, even an India favored in British capital markets, received very little investment. Simple two-factor models suggesting income equalization through capital and trade flows are inappropriate to the 19th-century reality. . . .

Revenue Finance

As London increasingly financed peripheral extension and trade expansion, Paris and Berlin focused instead on financing government expenditures in Eastern and Central Europe and the Middle East. Half of their portfolios on the eve of war were composed of European securities. Of the rest, Turkey (and for France, Egypt also) made up a sizable part. Rondo Cameron gives more detail for the French holdings: 25 percent in Russia, 4 percent in the Balkans, 12 percent in the Near East, 8 percent in Central Europe, 12 percent in Italy, Spain, and Portugal. Feis's estimates of the German distribution still remain as good as any: Russia, 8 percent; the Balkans, 7 percent; Turkey, 8 percent; Central Europe, 13 percent; and Spain and Portugal, 7 percent.

But the similarity of these static proportions is deceptive on two counts. First, Germany did not participate to the same degree as France in the boom of 1900–13, for domestic financing requirements dominated. Second, German enthusiasm for financing its immediate neighbors diminished in favor of investment in Latin America and of colonial undertakings in China and Africa. As holdings in Austria-Hungary, Rumania, and Russia stagnated or declined, Germany made its only new large European commitments in Turkey.

Revenue, as opposed to developmental, lending characterized these portfolios. Borrowing was more often to balance government accounts than to undertake infrastructure investment. Frequently it was occasioned by the need to fund a growing floating debt that had in the interim financed deficits on current account. While national debt grew as a liability, on the asset side there was nothing. In a moment of unusual jocularity, M. G. Mulhall recorded in the national balance sheet for Egypt a large equalizing sum for "ballet dancers, etc.," an item that exceeded the outlay for public works. More soberly, the financial report filed by Stephen Cave in 1876 pointed out "that for the present large amount of indebtedness there is absolutely nothing to show but the Suez Canal, the whole proceeds of the loans and floating debt having been absorbed in payment of interest and sinking funds."

Unproductive borrowing was, however, very profitable lending. The commissions to be gained were large and guaranteed, and in addition a potential for speculative capital gains existed if the debentures increased in price. Issue prices were set much below par in order to market them, and values of 60 to 70 percent of par were not uncommon. Even at such rates of interest to purchasers and despite the pledge of specific sources of state revenues (among them customs, land-holdings, and other natural resources), willing takers could not always be found. Then short-term finance would require even higher rates for the issuing bankers while efforts were undertaken to persuade the public of the soundness of another issue.

Getting the money was for borrowers frequently a Pyrrhic victory. The considerable cost of funds, which had no corresponding domestic application in productive assets, required increases in domestic revenues that were not always forthcoming, requiring loans to meet the interest on the previous debt. Borrowers were very much in a debt trap. At some point, and usually after a sustained upsurge in foreign investment had petered out, default was a likely outcome. Explicit hypothecation of public revenues and resources set the stage for outright intervention, to reform the offending state and to guarantee the repayment of interest.

This lending to governments had its institutional counterpart in a regulated capital market. Private investment decisions, in the absence of favorable real economic prospects, could not be relied upon to produce the desired outcome. High returns could work only for a short while, and thereafter the greater the private gain, the higher the probability of government default. Even bankers who initially profited at the expense of weakened nations eventually required some way to dispose of their overextended holdings. Default could become for them a source of gain rather than of loss, but only when some implicit guarantee of intervention promised to bring order to the financial chaos of mismanaged states and lead to refunding of prior debt. Public assurances that supported the continued lending required to avert default could work equally well. Both circumstances qualify David Landes's judgment that the "great international bankers . . . have always understood that prosperous, independent states make the best clients." . . .

Developmental and Public Revenue Defaults

Capital markets did not operate smoothly before 1914. Lenders and borrowers conducted their activities against the backdrop of large cyclical swings in international economic performance. Rebellion and war superimposed political shocks on economic fluctuations.

Part of the task of the capital market was to cope with periodic failures to meet contractual obligations.

The failures, like the motivations for lending, took two basic forms that required and received different treatment. On the one hand were developmental defaults: the counterpart debt of rapid investment in physical assets created temporary service burdens that exceeded capacity to pay. On the other were public-sector insolvencies, the result of a slowing in continuing capital flows that had hitherto financed the shortfall between government expenditures and revenues.

Countries experiencing developmental default showed rising exports and government revenues, were attractive to foreign investment in private undertakings in addition to public securities, paid moderate rates of interest, and were integrated into the world economy. Public-sector insolvency plagued stagnating economies whose governments financed current outlays with loans that they were able to get by paying exorbitantly high interest rates even while they were benefiting from temporarily favorable conditions of capital supply. Private securities were not issued.

The two modes of default shared a sensitivity to variation in foreign investment and a governmental inability to pay, but there the similarity ends. Developmental default governments could not pay because their revenues, closely tied to imports, declined sharply as slowing exports and capital inflows reduced import capacity. Investment was sensitive to performance, and the descent was self-reinforcing. Inflationary finance bid up the exchange rate and the cost of the required foreign exchange while discouraging new capital flows; even noninflationary finance could not help, since limited foreign exchange necessarily elevated the real debt burden. Such countries had a transfer problem.

The appropriate remedy was time: time for exports to rise and to increase internal prosperity, imports, and governmental revenues. Investment bankers helped provide that time in funding loans that consolidated debt and allowed for brief periods of reduced, or no, interest payments and amortization. With recovery, new loans would again flow, for the capital market bore no long-lasting grudge. In the interim there would be periods of export surplus and slowed domestic expansion. Development default was part of the long-swing pattern of peripheral expansion.

Revenue default was part of the same pattern, but more incidentally: it was linked through the conditions of access to capital markets. As flows diminished, so did capability to meet service payments. Investment had started in the first place because, with little debt, there were relatively large revenues to cover obligations. But interest costs rose more rapidly than revenues, soon eroding that initial capability. Revenue default was a case of genuine insolvency, with the interest cost on resources actually received after discounts far exceeding revenue growth. Little, if any, real resource transfer occurred. Lending might be sustained, but it was for political rather than for long-range economic reasons. And default might even be welcomed as a way of enhancing political influence.

The solution for revenue defaults was frequently drastic. By the 1870s it involved direct intervention to overhaul both public finances and public administration. Debt was significantly written down, either through much reduced interest payments or through lowered capital values (or both). Balancing such generosity was the assignment and sometimes even the external collection of the revenues required to service the debt. Latin America in the 1820s escaped such a fate despite a spate of public-sector insolvencies, because British policy of the time emphasized nonintervention. (Britain's position would change with time and the strategic location of the defaulter.) Instead, Latin American borrowing was precluded for almost fifty years and only resumed after settlements, sometimes costly ones.

These two types of default and their solutions flowed naturally from the distinctive lending processes inherent in the operation of the pre-1914 capital market. . . .

The two categories differ obviously in the composition of their foreign capital. Developmental borrowers, even when governmental participation was important (as in Australia, Argentina, and Brazil), attracted investment in complementary activities. Revenue borrowers, with the partial exception of Russia, did not. Such additional inflows tended to increase the ratios of foreign capital to exports for developmental borrowers. Yet their service payments are not correspondingly higher, because of the lower interest rates and smaller amortization charges that derive from longer-term debt. . . .

For the revenue borrowers, the ratio of public debt to revenues tends to be higher. . . . Correspondingly, the service requirements from public receipts are even greater because of the high interest costs on even the nominal values of the debt.

Development borrowers are further distinguished by their higher growth rates of exports and revenues and by their greater variance. The last is what gets them into trouble and provokes inability to pay. After a settlement is reached, they grow out of their problem and return to the good graces of the financial community. Revenue borrowers have indifferent export performance both before and after default; their economies are not significantly integrated into the world economy. Nor do revenues pick up significantly, despite interventions in Turkey, Egypt, and Greece. Creditors must simply settle for less because of the insolvency of the borrowers, and payments are reduced to conform with the debtors' capacity to pay.

The typical developmental default story, then, is one of export growth rates that immediately prior to the default are variable and lower than previously. At the same time foreign investment slows. The balance-of-payments problem translates into a public finance problem and eventually governmental default. After a settlement provides temporary relief, export growth and public revenues recover, investment resumes, and creditors eventually accept even higher ratios of capital to exports.

The typical revenue default is provoked by slowing inflows of capital that no longer obscure the underlying insolvency of interest rates, and hence inertial debt growth, higher than either export or revenue growth. Even when revenue growth had been strong, it was the consequence of exceptional resources — guano — or new taxes, neither of which could be projected to continue. With no expectation of recovery, radical solutions are necessary to reduce debt service. Since debt had initially been sold at substantial discount, a ready expedient is available: nominal debt can be scaled down in exchange for direct assignment and collection of revenues adequate to yield some low but potentially increasing return.

Did the Gold Standard Work as Advertised?

ALEC FORD

The growth of the export economies in Latin America in the second half of the nineteenth century required access to ample supplies of labor and capital. Bringing goods to market, for example, required transportation and port facilities, whose costs were exceptionally large. Railroads alone required investment in track, terminals, and rolling stock that went well beyond what domestic savers could accumulate. As a result, the role of foreign investment, especially direct investment in productive assets, assumed critical importance in financing economic growth.

The single largest source of foreign finance in Latin America was Great Britain, whose investments in Latin America by World War I were as large as those of France and Germany combined. About 20 percent of Britain's overseas investment was in Latin America, a percentage slightly greater than its investment in the United States. By comparison, about a third of German overseas investment and about 13 percent of French foreign investment were in Latin America. Great Britain had become the world's international financial leader during the Napoleonic Wars, and for the next century, until World War I, London was the world's leading financial center. British investments largely flowed to Brazil and Argentina, but the mineral resources of Mexico, Chile, Bolivia, Peru, and Colombia were extracted with the aid of foreign capital. Most of the Argentine rail network was financed by British and French capital. Coffee, cotton, and flour processing in Brazil was largely underwritten by British investment.

A key element in the movement of foreign capital to Latin America was the gold standard, a system of financial arrangements in which national currencies were defined in terms of gold. In this way, the price of one currency in terms of another, known as the exchange rate, was quite predictable. Stable exchange rates make international investment more attractive because they reduce the risk to investors from changes in the value of another

Alec Ford, "Notes on the Working of the Gold Standard Before 1914," *Oxford Economic Papers*, (1960), 61–65, 72–73, 74–76. Reprinted by permission of Oxford University Press, England.

currency. The gold standard has been the subject of great historical interest, because its smooth operation was considered "automatic." Under the gold standard, a country's balance of trade was said to determine its domestic money supply, and hence its level of prices. Surpluses or deficits in the balance of trade would produce offsetting changes in the money supply, and these changes, in turn, would restore equilibrium to a country's international position.

In practice, the operation of the gold standard was considerably more complex. Great Britain could moderate the effects of surpluses or deficits on its money supply, because the Bank of England could reduce or raise interest rates. But for countries in Latin America, none of which had genuine central banks, the system operated differently. As Alec Ford illustrates in this classic article, countries such as Argentina could not stop the loss of gold (and hence a contraction in its money supply) by borrowing more. Argentina and Chile, whose economic cycles were tied to commodity exports, experienced large inflows of gold as their exports swelled, so that prices and employment became unstable.

Moreover, as Ford points out, the position of export-oriented elites in Argentina complicated the political dimensions of international adjustment. During a boom, landowners whose products were exported profited from falling exchange rates, because their receipts in gold purchased more domestic currency. But as growth slowed, a rise in the exchange rate worked against them and made abandoning the gold standard more attractive.

In other words, although the gold standard facilitated the movement of capital to countries such as Argentina and Chile, its purported stabilizing effects on their economics are difficult to determine. Yet there was no sense in which trade and investment impoverished the Argentine economy, as some versions of dependency thinking hold. Rather, foreign capital made a significant contribution to the growth of the countries that received it, but at the cost of exaggerated economic and political instability.

Alec Ford is the author of *The Gold Standard, 1880–1914: Britain and Argentina* (1962) and "International Financial Policy and the Gold Standard, 1870–1914," in *The Cambridge Economic History of Europe,* Volume VIII (1989).

Argentina, of vast land area and with various climates and vegetations, and sparsely populated, advanced rapidly as a primary producer in the nineteenth century as transport barriers were removed. The federal constitution, adopted in 1862, resembled the American, but gave much more power to the President, whilst the dominant political group was the conservative landowning (and export-producing) oligarchy, whose rule was maintained until 1910 either by fraud or by force at the 'free' elections. The fact that power was seated here will enable us to understand certain economic actions of the national governments.

Export values expanded sevenfold within the period 1880–1913, and their composition changed sharply, the main exports in 1880 being wool, fleeces, and hides, whilst after 1890 grains (i.e. wheat, maize, linseed) rose in importance. The twentieth century saw the decline of sheep farming and the rapid rise of cattle ranching and export of frozen beef. It is important to note that Argentina was a relatively small *producer* of these products, whose prices were determined in centralized commodity markets, and thus she had little or no control over her export prices. Additionally, Argentina was heavily dependent on export sales for her well-being, since roughly half of her primary produce was exported. Imports, which expanded six times in value, were composed of food, drink, tobacco, manufactures of all kinds, fuel, machinery and rails, whilst their prices were largely determined by suppliers, since Argentina was a relatively small part of the world market for these products. Moreover, since Argentine production comprised exportable goods mainly and little import-competing industry existed, there was little substitution between home-produced and imported goods.

Foreign investment by European centres — especially London — together with immigration, from Italy and Spain particularly, had brought about this expansion with the railway as the basic factor which had permitted this 'export-biased' development to take place. Other important destinations of foreign funds were governmental borrowings, public utilities, land mortgage bonds, tramways and land companies. One important consequence of this borrowing must be noted — the foreign debt-service charges incurred had a large element fixed and payable in gold or sterling.

The domestic currency, the paper peso (a gold peso was an oddity), had a history of depreciation in the nineteenth century, whilst Argentine banking was anarchic, there being no central bank, although in later years after 1900 the Bank of the Nation tended to be dominant through sheer size. The commercial banks were sharply divided into international banks, based on other monetary centres, which specialized in foreign trade and remittance business, and domestic banks, which looked to local business. Argentina, however, hardly belonged to the English monetary area, as much of the banking system was purely local.

In summary, then, Argentina was an economy predominantly dependent on the production of exportables and the level of foreign-currency receipts for the determining of her income and well-being. Her export and import prices together with prices of domestically consumed exportables were determined externally, whilst there was low substitutability between imports and home-produced non-exportables, so that the scope for price changes to promote balance-of-payments adjustment was severely limited. Furthermore, fluctuations in foreign-currency receipts provided the principal cause not only of fluctuations in income, but also of balance-of-payments disequilibria, so that in this setting the question 'Why did gold move?' is to be answered frequently by pointing to changes in export proceeds or in the flow of funds from abroad. Changes in either of these variables brought directly associated income movements and hence equilibrating changes in import purchases.

In 1881 monetary reforms were enacted in Argentina to remedy the previously chaotic condition of the currency; the main provisions were the definition of the new gold peso, the replacement of the existing paper currencies by a new national paper peso (at par with the gold peso) whose issue by approved banks was subject to regulation by the national government, and the convertibility of paper pesos into gold. In 1883 these were put into operation and Argentina had *formally* rejoined the gold standard. Yet the internal banking system, although sizeable, was rudimentary, whilst the foreign-based banks were not dominant nor did they hold the major part of the Argentine gold and foreign-exchange reserves. This situation may be contrasted with the institutional arrangements prevailing in New Zealand and Australia, for example, where overseas banks did provide considerable internal facilities and where London branches (or head offices) held the countries' foreign-exchange reserves in the form of sterling balances. Sanctions on excessive note issue were weak; indeed the country had a tradition of these being ignored or removed by governments in difficulties, as indeed it had a tradition of depreciated paper money, so that popular confidence in the stability of the paper peso–gold peso link was not high.

Furthermore, the dominant political interests, the export producers and landowners, were not adversely affected by a depreciating exchange; rather a depreciating exchange shifted the distribution of a given real income in their favour whilst an appreciating exchange moved it against them. For, with constant world prices, depreciation increased the paper peso prices of exportables *pari passu,* and hence producers' receipts in paper currency for a given output. Wage-rates (both urban and rural), however, were sluggish, showing no comparable increase, and the landowners' mortgage debts were for the most part fixed in terms of paper currency, so that the gap between their receipts and costs widened by more than the depreciation. On the other hand, an appreciating exchange rate with constant world prices cut the paper prices of exportable produce *pari passu,* shifted the income distribution in favour of wage-earners, for wages were 'sticky' in paper currency, and increased the real burden of a given paper peso debt for landowners. Lastly, less moral shame (such as prevailed widely in Britain) was felt at a depreciating exchange. Accordingly, it is not surprising to find in times of balance-of-payments deficit a bias in favour of a depreciating exchange rate, and in times of persistent surplus a distinct preference for a stable exchange rate rather than an appreciating rate. Indeed, these effects are of the utmost importance in explaining Argentina's lapse from the gold standard in 1885 and her decision to rejoin in 1900.

With this background it would be reasonable to expect that a small disturbance in the balance of payments, which an older member of the gold standard club could have withstood either from its own resources or by means of short-term foreign loans, might have more serious repercussions. Any sustained export of gold would provoke internal speculation, the populace becoming bulls of gold, and thus the note-issuing banks' gold reserves (in any case none too plentiful) would be subjected to a further drain as gold was absorbed into private hoards in the expectation of a breakdown of the system and the emergence of a gold premium.

Indeed, as early as January 1885 a gold premium had appeared despite the attempts of the issuing banks to preserve paper convertibility at par. In their attempts the Banco Nacional and the Bank of the Province of Buenos Aires had lost 77 million pesos worth of gold and foreign exchange, of which the major share, perhaps 50 million pesos, was absorbed *internally,* the rest internationally. The international drain in 1884 had arisen because the proceeds of foreign borrowing declined whilst imports and foreign debt-service charges had increased and exports barely expanded—these items giving rise to a deficit of 14 million pesos, as compared with a surplus of 7 million in 1883. Doubtless this drain encouraged some domestic speculative hoarding of gold, but this is not the whole story, for as early as June 1884 the Bank of the Province of Buenos Aires suspended specie payments. This would seem early for international forces to have made their impact; rather, one suspects, it was the victim of some autonomous domestic speculation, perhaps even a deliberate run on gold by special interests who stood to gain by the emergence of a gold premium. Domestic lack of confidence, justified by precedent, was the first cause of Argentina's withdrawal from the gold standard. The second was the lack of any institutional mechanism for coping with a balance-of-payments deficit by short-term capital movements and in the longer run by credit contraction. This illustrates a previous theme: a creditor (lending) country can always—easily—bring relief to its balance of payments by lending less abroad; a debtor (borrowing) country will find it hard or even impossible to bring relief by borrowing more—the more so if it has a history of currency depreciation and is thus 'suspect' internationally. Yet to some extent similar economic conditions prevailed in other primary producing countries and exchange stability was preserved before 1914. More, indeed, depended on social, political, and moral attitudes to exchange stability, on the structure of society and the political system, and on tradition. . . .

The difficulties which a primary producing country, heavily dependent on export sales for its prosperity, may experience in maintaining exchange stability, are well known, and in Argentina were aggravated by her international debtor status; a debtor has service charges, which for Argentina had a large core fixed in gold or sterling and formed a considerable item in her foreign-currency payments. Further, in times of world depression or adversity there was a tendency for short-term funds to move back to creditor countries and away from debtors, irrespective of the latter's interest rates—a movement which affected Argentina especially keenly because of the lack of international confidence in the peso. Thus no short-term capital movements served to soften the export of gold, which had to be staunched speedily by income movements if exchange stability was to be preserved.

Again, Argentina illustrates the weakness for an 'export' economy where the quantity of money is determined by international gold and foreign-currency movements, in that booms and slumps generally arose because of changes in foreign-currency receipts which also brought imports or exports of gold as well so that the initial income movements were exaggerated by changes in liquidity. It was thus difficult to accumulate a sufficient gold reserve during a boom to cope with bad times — apart from the itching palm of some early Argentine governments for idle gold! Furthermore, the fact that in years of depression the initial contractive effects were intensified by monetary factors tended to alienate support for the gold standard system. This is quite different from the cases of some other countries where booms and slumps originated for domestic reasons and met with a fairly stable monetary supply so that rising or falling interest rates tended to mitigate these initial income movements. Here booms were associated with adverse balances of payments, slumps with favourable balances so that the monetary policy dictated by gold movements tended to lessen (not enhance) income fluctuations and the gold standard system was more acceptable than in the former case.

These economic difficulties which might have sufficed in themselves to render adherence to the gold standard impossible, were supplemented by political and social factors which in the last resort proved decisive. The domestic convertibility of notes for gold, which was the prime object for Britain and certain other economies and from which the international gold standard sprang, was not such a point of honour and morality. Other primary producers, such as Australia and New Zealand, maintained exchange-rate stability, which is explained by different administrative and political systems with different social structures, and by their banking systems being based on London. However, in Argentina, aided by the particular economic and political structure, the landed and export-producing oligarchy willingly abandoned or adopted the gold standard system whenever it was to their benefit and profit. . . .

The following crude pattern of economic relationships between Britain and the primary producers who were on the periphery of the gold standard system suggests itself. British loans to overseas countries increased their purchases from Britain and their debt-service payments so that on the one hand they did not permanently gain much gold, nor did Britain lose much gold through the loan-transfer transactions. Secondly, when the investment projects matured, their production of exportables was expanded, for which there was a ready market in Britain. The primary producers' exports rose so that they could pay their foreign debt-service charges and dividend remittances, *and* purchase more imports, whilst because of their growing prosperity British exports expanded. Such trade flows thus contributed to the economic growth of both partners and their mutual welfare, besides providing a basis for stability.

This idyllic scheme, although perhaps realized pretty well in the long run, did give rise to particular short-run difficulties especially for the primary producers. For, in the upsurge of foreign lending if the sums transferred were temporarily in excess of Britain's current-account surplus and caused the loss of gold, Bank Rate adjustments and the reflux of British short-term funds brought speedy relief. On the other hand, the decline in foreign lending often occurred before the investment projects had been completed and had expanded exportable production so that balance-of-payments difficulties faced the borrowers because of the added burden of extra debt-service charges on an as yet unexpanded production — especially if the ratio of debt-service charges/exports had risen sharply. In this setting of crisis (and possible British fears about these countries' exchange stability or possible default on interest payments) it is dubious whether the short-term pool of credit in London helped such economies to the extent that has sometimes been suggested. Rather they were left to adjust themselves through income movements, which affected their import purchases, whether they remained on the gold standard or perforce embraced a system of flexible exchange rates.

Again, variations in the prices of primary products and in the terms of trade tended to affect these economies more sharply than Britain, for they were more heavily dependent on international trade in most cases. Indeed, in the short run sharp fluctuations impeded or enhanced development, and brought in the former case balance-of-payments strain. For example, falling primary product prices between 1889 and 1896 prevented Argentine export values from rising, despite a great expansion in the volume of exportable production which foreign investment had facilitated; after 1896, however, rising prices enhanced export values, facilitated greatly her return to the gold standard in 1900 and her subsequent adherence until 1914.

How British Capital Sustained Argentine Growth

ALAN M. TAYLOR

In the half century after the fall of the regional autocrat Juan Manuel de Rosas in 1852, Argentina underwent a dramatic transformation. Past political conflicts were settled, and the economy was transformed. Substantial inflows of British capital (and after 1900, French and German too) and massive immigration, mostly by Italians and Spaniards, drove the creation of an export economy whose growth was nothing if not spectacular. Exports of wool, wheat, and corn, brought to market by an extensive railroad system, increased rapidly down to 1900, after which chilled beef played a major role as well. In 1870, Argentina ranked eleventh in world per capita income.

Yet the Argentine story since 1930 has been considerably less fortunate. Growth slowed dramatically, and today Argentina's per capita income is not even in the world's top fifty. Numerous explanations have been proposed for Argentina's progressive impoverishment, ranging from the economic decline of Argentina's best export customer, Great Britain, to a shift to inward-looking, relatively inefficient import-substitution industrialization, to class conflict and political instability, which made economic populism attractive.

Alan Taylor offers an intriguing contribution to the debate. Although historians like David Rock have sometimes argued that Argentina's poor twentieth-century performance can be traced to insufficient savings, Taylor tackles the question from a somewhat different angle. Argentina's heavy immigration, he argues, led to rapid population growth—in other words, a country with more dependent children. But a younger population is less able and less likely to save, because its earning capacity is limited, even as its needs for food, clothing, and shelter grow. As long as Britain could finance Argentine investment, Argentina could continue to grow. But after World War I, the chief source of overseas invest-

Alan M. Taylor, "External Dependence, Demographic Burdens, and Argentine Economic Decline after the Belle Époque," *The Journal of Economic History,* 52: 4 (1992), pp. 907–911, 920–921, 928–929. Reprinted by permission of Cambridge University Press.

ment was no longer Britain, but the United States. And the United States, for whatever reasons, was less willing to lend than Great Britain had been, a fact that contemporaries did not fail to notice. In any event, Taylor neatly turns one notion of dependency on its head. Foreign investment did not exploit Argentina. Rather, foreign investment made rapid Argentine growth up to World War I possible. Taylor does not explicitly consider Alec Ford's arguments in his paper, but it is worth considering the contrast implicit in their views of the impact of the gold standard on Argentine growth in the years before World War I.

The record of Argentine economic performance tells a story of decline unparalleled in modern times. The country has endured a painful adjustment to the end of the *Belle Époque,* a glittering period in its history that reached its peak early this century. A visitor to Buenos Aires then would have marveled at the splendors of the city: the impressive opera house, the graceful architecture, the sophisticated railway system. Today the city presents the same elegant façade, only frayed and decaying at the edges—and the visitor marvels that the city can function at all, given its dilapidated infrastructure. The satisfaction of living in one of the richest countries in the world is now a distant memory for the Argentines, who have struggled to come to terms with their sinking status. The downfall of this once developed country is as much of an enigma for students of economic history, and the contradictions between her past success and current failure constitute "one of the most puzzling and misunderstood national stories in the development literature." . . .

What, then, marked the end of the *Belle Époque*: the Great War or the Great Depression? Few of the protagonists in the debate can agree on the timing, let alone the mechanisms of Argentine economic growth—but all agree that the country in some sense failed. For the development economist it is enlightening, even uplifting, to study national success cases: to try to figure out what went right and how those lessons can be applied elsewhere. Yet the study of economic failure, though depressing, can be a revealing exercise. More compelling and mysterious examples of failure than the ruination of Argentina are hard to imagine. An array of intriguing questions presents itself: When did the tables turn? How dramatic was the decline? What was the basis of the previous success? Why did it disappear?

To answer these questions we must first assess the quantitative record of Argentine growth in an international perspective. The issue of long-run economic development and the relative performance of different countries has recently come under close scrutiny. In the historical arena, the work of Angus Maddison, William Baumol, Bradford De Long, and other investigators has offered us a detailed perspective on trends in growth performance over the last 100 years or more. In this spirit I will now review the irregular record of Argentine performance in a comparative setting. Of particular interest is the common comparison of Argentina with the other settler economies, Australia and Canada, and the measure of Argentine performance relative to the larger OECD group of now developed countries.

The relative economic performance of Argentina in the twentieth century is summarized in the table. The picture presented there immediately begins to unravel the confusion in the debate over Argentine failure: one's view of relative Argentine retardation depends entirely on the basis of the comparison. Australia and Canada performed dismally in the interwar period, undergoing retardation relative to the OECD group as a whole (their ratio of income per capita relative to the OECD average fell from 1913 to 1929); in that context, Argentine performance looks respectable. Furthermore, the table illustrates that the post-1913 retardation was much more serious in the settler economies (ranging from 1.59 to 2.23 percentage points) than in the OECD (0.25). In a sense, Díaz-Alejandro is right to praise Argentina for keeping pace with the other settler economies; but keeping pace with stragglers is no great feat. In fact, the settler economies were hit much harder than almost any other country by the economic shocks associated with the Great War, as seen in Maddison's full sample of 28 countries (see panel C). It is striking that among the five hardest hit countries, three were settler economies.

Thus a comparison of just the settler economies is misleading, tending to mutual flattery among a group of poor performers. The table provides the more reliable large-sample comparison we seek with the OECD. Australia and Canada have generally been leaders in the group, with income per capita above the OECD average. Australia has tended to converge down toward the OECD average, and Canada, if anything, to diverge upward. Since 1913 the ratio of Argentine per capita income to the OECD average has diverged mo-

Comparative Economic Growth

	1900	1913	1929	1950	1973	1987
A. GDP per Capita (international dollars, 1980 prices)						
Argentina	1,284	1,770	2,036	2,324	3,713	3,302
Australia	2,923	3,390	3,146	4,389	7,696	9,533
Canada	1,808	2,773	3,286	4,822	9,350	12,702
OECD	1,817	2,224	2,727	3,553	7,852	10,205
B. GDP per Capita (relative to OECD = 1.00)						
Argentina	0.71	0.80	0.75	0.65	0.47	0.32
Australia	1.61	1.52	1.15	1.24	0.98	0.93
Canada	1.00	1.25	1.20	1.36	1.19	1.24

C. Growth Rates of GDP per Capita (%)

	1900–1913 (1)	1913–1929 (2)	Retardation (1) – (2)
Argentina	2.47	0.88	1.59
Australia	1.14	−0.47	1.61
Canada	3.29	1.06	2.23
OECD sample	1.55	1.27	0.25 [0.95][a]
28-country sample	1.34	1.02	0.33 [0.98][a]

[a]This denotes a sample average, with the standard deviation shown in brackets.

Note: Panel B is derived from Panel A.

SOURCES: Maddison, *The World Economy in the 20th Century* (Paris: OECD, 1989), p. 19.

notonically downward and away from parity; based on this evidence, the early-retardation hypothesis gains credence. Argentina, after all, aspired to membership in the club of developed countries—yet, when compared over the long run with levels of OECD performance, *the closest it came was in 1913. . . .*

The assertion that Argentine retardation commenced with the Great War is supported by quantitative evidence from a number of different sources. In terms of per capita income, it was at this time that Argentina started to lag behind the developed countries in growth performance. Even more telling, Argentina failed to advance capital deepening relative to Australia, itself a disaster case in terms of interwar retardation and slow growth.

I will argue that the retardation can best be understood in terms of Argentina's historically determined position on the eve of the Great War, in terms of both population structure and foreign capital dependence. Faster population growth, with more fecund and numerous immigrants, tended to burden Argentina demographically, not simply in terms of capital widening but in terms of a high dependency rate. Populous young cohorts threaten growth to the extent that their consumption needs diminish savings, with a carry-over effect in investment and accumulation. Admittedly, savings shortfall did not prove bothersome to Argentina before 1913. Under the stability of the gold standard ample flows of foreign investment could be attracted and domestic investment sustained. A high-immigration and high-overseas-borrowing strategy *could* work in a liberal world order characterized by free migration and internationally mobile capital.

Unfortunately, such a growth strategy was destined to grind to a halt, given its vulnerability to the economic shocks precipitated by the Great War. Whereas a temporary squeeze in commodity markets had to be endured, the severe squeeze in factor markets was permanent. Although labor migration recovered somewhat, the Great War wrought wholesale changes in the operation of international capital markets. In addition to the general retreat of all countries into a more autarkic stance, the keeper of the gold standard was unable to preserve its role intact. War debts had bankrupted Britain, who, bailed out by the United States, emerged from the war unable to continue playing the role of banker to the world.

The sudden scarcity of funds had profound implications for those nations heavily dependent on British finance, although the impact varied from country to country. Foreign ownership of Argentine capital measured in real terms reached its peak in 1913; in contrast, Australian capital inflows continued to mount through the interwar period. Note also the retreat of foreign capital from Argentina: foreign owners held 47.7 percent of the Argentine capital stock of 1913, but the foreign ownership share declined throughout the interwar period to a mere 20.4 percent in 1940. During this phase, net real additions to the Argentine capital stock were funded entirely by domestic accumulation. . . .

Measured by almost any standards, Argentine economic decline set in after the Great War—only a comparison with the other struggling settler economies can make Argentina's interwar economic performance look respectable. It would be unreasonable, however, to expect a single story to underlie this phenomenon, and this article only offers a partial accounting for the decades of poor Argentine economic performance. In doing so it highlights the difficult transition to the interwar period. One distinctive feature of the early-twentieth-century Argentine economy was its remarkably low savings capacity compared with Canada and Australia. Untroubled by low rates of domestic accumulation, Argentina flourished during the *Belle Époque* prior to 1913: foreign borrowing, principally in the London capital market, financed a rapidly growing capital stock, and rates of capital deepening and income growth made Argentina one of the fastest-growing economies of the day.

External dependence on foreign capital was crucial in Argentina because of the scarcity of domestic capital, which resulted in large part from demographic constraints on domestic savings. A high dependency rate, driven by a fast-growing population and substantial immigration, gave rise to an age structure with a large share of young dis-savers. The shortfall in available investable resources had to be made up by capital inflows—what Jeffrey Williamson and I viewed as an intergenerational transfer from mature savers in the Old World.

When international capital flows were cut off, following the collapse of the international capital market and Britain's retreat into debtor status, the balance-of-payments gap could be bridged no longer, and the demographic burden forestalled Argentine accumulation through the interwar period. Counterfactual analysis demonstrates that under more forgiving circumstances—a lower dependency rate comparable to those of the other settler economies—Argentine interwar performance would have been close to the average for the rest of the world economy.

In the development literature, much ink has been spilled in discussing the obstacle that external dependence presents to a developing country, and the need for self-sufficiency and delinking from the core group of industrial nations; such arguments usually fall under the controversial rubric of dependency theory. Díaz-Alejandro offered a scathing critique of such inward-looking approaches to development in his influential article "Delinking North and South: Unshackled or Unhinged?" In the context of Argentine economic

decline, I have sought to show that another kind of dependency burden, of the demographic variety, can render external dependence in
capital markets a vital underpinning to the development process.
British capital paid for a *Belle Époque* that the young Argentine
population could not underwrite alone: delinked from this external
market Argentina became not unshackled but, indeed, unhinged.

Brazilian Industry
and the Great Depression

STEPHEN H. HABER

Stephen H. Haber is the author of *Industry and Underdevelopment: The Industrialization of Mexico, 1890–1940* (1989). In the
article excerpted here, Haber questions a common assumption of
dependency writing. Writers such as André Gunder Frank have
suggested that times of international crisis could be beneficial to
"peripheral" or "underdeveloped" areas in the international economy. They reason that interruptions in the flow of manufactured
goods from the developed economies (provoked, for example, by
warfare or commercial depression) create opportunities for the
production of substitute goods in the peripheral economies. Alter-
natively, a rise in commodity prices occasioned by military demands (such as the rise in the price of henequen fibers from Yucatán during World War I) would also prove helpful.

In looking at textile manufacturing in Brazil during the Great
Depression, Haber finds something rather different. According to
Haber, the Great Depression hit Brazilian manufacturing hard.
Economic historians who have in the past relied on highly aggre-
gated statistics have been misled, Haber suggests. Haber's study
focuses less on industry-wide statistics (for instance, industrial
censuses or excise tax records) than on the study of representative
firms. As a result, the picture he presents is rather more subtle, for
there was considerable variation among firms, and changes in a

Excerpts from Stephen H. Haber, "Business Enterprise and the Great Depression in
Brazil: A Study of Profits and Losses in Textile Manufacturing," *Business History
Review*, Summer 1992, pp. 335–338, 351–353, 362–363. Copyright © 1992 by the
President and Fellows of Harvard College. Reprinted by permission of Harvard Busi-
ness School.

firm's profitability did not always vary in the same way as changes in production. For purposes of comparison, one might read Albert Fishlow's "Origins and Consequences of Import Substitution in Brazil," (1972) in which Fishlow concludes that import substitution in Brazil during the Great Depression "gave an impulse to the evolution of a more sophisticated productive structure." Haber's conclusions are quite different.

The role of the Great Depression in fostering (or hindering) Latin American industrialization is part of a broader discussion on the relationship between instability in the international economy and growth and development in Latin American economies. The current view is that the Great Depression of the 1930s did not lead to a decisive advance in Latin American industrialization. Yet the effects of earlier shocks as varied as the commercial depression of the seventeenth century; the Napoleonic Wars (1793–1815); the financial crises of 1825 and 1837; the Crimean War (1856–1857); the United States Civil War (1861–1865); the Baring Crisis (1890); and World War I (1914–1918) have not, and obviously cannot, produce similar consensus. For a provocative discussion of some of these episodes, see Colin Lewis, "Industry in Latin America before 1930," in Leslie Bethell, ed., *The Cambridge History of Latin America* (Volume 4, 1986).

During the 1980s, economic historians of Latin America have turned their attention increasingly to the impact of the Great Depression. The numerous studies of the larger economies of the region indicate that the course of the Great Depression in Latin America was significantly different from that in the United States and Western Europe. In this view, the Depression began quite a bit earlier in Latin America than in the advanced industrial economies, but it was a good deal less severe. Moreover, the recovery from the Depression was rapid: the larger economies of the region were on the rebound by 1933 and then grew at impressive rates throughout the rest of the decade. Finally, the literature suggests that during the period of recovery the engine of growth shifted from primary products to manufacturing: import-substituting industry outgrew the traditional export sector.

With few exceptions, these earlier studies have been based almost entirely on analyses of government revenues, foreign trade data, and aggregate indexes of manufacturing production derived from industrial censuses or published taxation records. We therefore know a good deal about the movement of aggregate economic indicators. Economies are not made up of statistical indexes, however, but rather of workers earning wages and capitalists earning profits. About the actual state of business enterprise during the Great Depression we know very little.

The use of aggregate data has three significant limitations. First, the economic statistics published by Latin American governments during the first part of the twentieth century are not particularly reliable or consistent in their coverage. The data on manufacturing are especially suspect, because the information was originally gathered for taxation purposes, which would not have encouraged bias-free responses from factory owners. In fact, in Brazil the first industrial census (1907) was carried out by the national manufacturers' association, because it was believed that industrialists would not respond to a survey conducted by the federal government. Second, there is not always a direct correlation between the level of output and the financial performance of an industry. These variables can, and often do, move in opposite directions. Third, sole reliance on aggregate indicators may mask substantial variations among different types of industries and firms.

The purpose of this article, therefore, is to shed some light on the effects of the Depression on manufacturing enterprise in Latin America by going beyond the aggregate statistics to look at the experience of individual enterprises. It concentrates on Brazil, which, in the period after the First World War, had the largest and most industrialized economy in the region. Within the manufacturing sector, this study focuses on the most significant and best-developed industry, cotton textiles. No other industry approached it in size, regional diversity, or backward linkages. At the time of Brazil's 1920 industrial census, cotton textiles accounted for 24.4 percent of manufacturing value added, second only to the food-processing industries, which accounted for 32.9 percent. Most food processing, however, consisted of preparing sugar and coffee for export and thus did not represent the same type of import-substituting manufacturing that textiles did. If these export-related processing industries are factored out, textiles accounted for just over one-third of Brazilian manufacturing.

The basic argument advanced here is that the Depression hit Brazilian manufacturing a good deal harder than the aggregate data indicate. Indeed, all three limitations of aggregate data operate in the Brazilian case to give a misleading picture of the Depression's effects on business enterprise. First, the coverage of the aggregate indicators is very irregular. The partial industrial census of 1907 was followed by a more complete census in 1920, but no other sector-wide manufacturing census was carried out until 1940, making a study of the Depression based on census data highly problematic. Researchers have relied, therefore, almost entirely on a production index derived from excise tax records. This series (as I shall discuss later) underestimates the impact of the Depression on the industry and overestimates the extent of the recovery. Second, firm profitability did not always move in the same direction as output. Third, there was a substantial variation among firms that is masked by the aggregate series. Indeed, some firms were pushed to the wall and underwent financial restructuring during the Depression, whereas others were turning phenomenal profits. These differences are largely attributable to the different entrepreneurial strategies followed by Brazil's mill owners before the Depression.

This article also argues that the Great Depression had important long-run consequences for the Brazilian textile industry. The analysis of the behavior of individual firms lends support to the argument made by Stanley Stein and Albert Fishlow that the Depression discouraged new investment and innovation in Brazil's consumer goods industries and that it ultimately worked to slow their rate of growth well after the Depression had ended. . . .

All three sets of estimates of the rate of return on capital indicate that the Brazilian cotton textile industry was in serious trouble before 1929. Median rates of return on capital stock fell steadily from 7 percent in the first semester of 1925 to 2 percent in the second semester of 1927. The depreciated rate of return on capital stock series displays a similar trend, with a decline from 3 percent to zero over the same period. Market rates of return were somewhat stickier, displaying almost no significant movement from 1925 to 1927. Firms depleted reserve funds in order to continue paying out dividends even when current profits did not support them. Thus, dividend payments as a percentage of par values did not decline as dramatically as did book value rates of return. Moreover, the market adjusted to the slightly lower dividend stream in 1926 and 1927 by bidding down the value of low-dividend company stock, thereby keeping the market rate of return constant. The result was a significant deterioration of the ratio of market to book values; the average of the index declined from 100 in 1925 to 62 in 1927.

By 1929, with reserve funds exhausted and revenues severely

depressed, most companies stopped paying dividends. The market rate of return now moved more in parallel with book value rates of return. The median book value rate of return on capital stock dropped to zero in the first semester of 1929 and stayed there through 1933, with the trough of –2 percent per semester reached in the second semester of 1931. The depreciated book value rate-of-return estimates tell the same story, though more dramatically. Profits fell from zero in the second semester of 1927 to –5 percent in the first semester of 1931, hovering in the negative range through 1933. From 1928 to 1933, the median overall losses would have been 33 percent. As profits disappeared and firms were forced to the wall, there was nothing, except bad news, to distribute to the investors. Median dividend payments as a percentage of paid-in capital had run between 3 and 8 percent per semester from 1925 to 1928; now they stood at zero. In 1929 only two firms managed to pay dividends, and by 1930 only one firm, São Pedro de Alcantara, continued to do so. That company alone managed to pay consistent dividends throughout the Depression; all the others ceased distributing profits to shareholders until the second semester of 1934 or paid dividends irregularly. Median market rates of return were therefore zero in four of the five years from 1929 to 1933. As in the early years of the Depression, the market compensated for lower dividend payments by bidding down stock prices. Thus, the index of market to book values, which had stood at 62 in 1927, fell steadily to 23 in 1930 and recovered only slightly (to 34) in 1933. . . .

The firm-level analysis presented here has a number of implications for the study of Latin American industrial development. First, the data developed lend support to the argument made by Stanley Stein that the recovery from the Depression in Brazil was not accompanied by a concomitant resurgence in new investment. Instead, as Stein has pointed out, Brazil's textile industrialists turned to the state to limit new competition by freezing machinery imports, making a program of new investment difficult if not impossible. Even as late as 1937, the Brazilian investment community still valued the assets of the textile industry at less than half their 1925 values.

Second, the analysis underlines the important role played by state intervention in Brazil's industrial development. The modern Brazilian textile industry owed much of its early success to protectionist measures designed to insulate it from foreign competition, as well as to government loans designed to prevent many of the major firms from going bankrupt in the credit crunch of the mid-1890s. In the 1920s, Brazil's textile industrialists chose once again in a time of trouble to turn to the state to structure the market, rather than to pursue a process of reinvestment and modernization in order to become internationally competitive. As Albert Fishlow has pointed out, this experience of the Depression encouraged a model of growth in the consumer goods industries based on the exploitation of vast amounts of inexpensive labor and encouraged a mindset of short-run planning and technological and managerial obsolescence. Over the long run, this strategy of capital-scarce industrialization perpetuated the use of antiquated technology and low-wage, labor-intensive methods of production. The strategy ultimately led "not to successful modernization, but to slow rates of growth and actual reduction of the initial labor force"in later decades once pressure for higher wages made the continuation of the labor-intensive strategy infeasible.

Third, judging by the Brazilian case, it appears that the Great Depression had a more profound impact on Latin American manufacturing than previously thought. Certainly, the analysis of the eight cotton textile firms studied here should not be regarded as conclusive evidence that the aggregate data for all product lines in all countries are flawed. But it does suggest that scholars should be wary of relying solely on published aggregate statistics in their analyses of Latin America's early industrial experience. Indeed, a similar firm-level analysis of the Mexican case indicates that its experience was not unlike Brazil's in terms of the timing, strength, and duration of the Depression.

The discrepancy between the published statistical series and the experience of individual firms suggests that scholars need to shift the unit of analysis from aggregate economic sectors to the individual business enterprise. The value of the firm perspective is further underlined when one considers the substantial variation in profitability among the firms measured here. Judging from this sample, those enterprises that invested in new plant and equipment during the early 1920s weathered the storm of the Depression much better than those that did not invest. Whether this was the case in all product lines or was peculiar to textiles bears examination. Why some firms followed investment and modernization strategies different from the norm is a question that deserves attention as well. Without studies that specify the individual business enterprise as the unit of analysis, however, these questions will remain unanswered.

PART IV

From Depression
to Import Substitution

If the years between 1870 and 1914 witnessed the rapid and thorough integration of Latin America into the world economy, the subsequent half century signaled the beginnings of a retreat. This occurred in large part because of the erosion of conditions that had favored the expansion of international trade in the nineteenth century. Analysts such as Barry Eichengreen and Carlos Marichal point in particular to the growing instability of commodity prices and interest rates, which made the international environment riskier. These changes were especially evident in fluctuations of the terms of trade for primary products, or the prices at which primary goods exchanged for manufactures. Although the terms of trade had been slowly declining since the 1870s, their fall after World War I was considerably sharper. They made a brief recovery in the mid-1920s, but by the latter part of the decade, the terms of trade had once again begun to fall. By the onset of the Great Depression, the terms of trade for primary products were perhaps no more than half what they had been in 1870. In these price movements, some analysts discern support for what is sometimes called export pessimism, and what in Latin America is frequently termed the Prebisch-Singer hypothesis. [For example, see John Spraos, "The Statistical Debate on the Net Barter Terms of Trade Between Primary Commodities and Manufactures," *The Economic Journal* (1980), and David Sapsford, "The Prebisch-Singer Terms of Trade Hypothesis: Some New Evidence," *Economics Letters* (1985)].

The Prebisch-Singer, or simply Prebisch, hypothesis represented a reaction to the liberal belief in the inevitably beneficial impact of trade and investment on Latin America. It suggested that the terms of trade for Latin America's primary commodities (measured against the prices of manufactured imports) would continue to deteriorate. In plain words, a country would have to run faster to stay in the same place. Exports did not represent a viable engine of economic growth over the long run. Moreover, flows of capital and merchandise were inherently unpredictable. International conflicts and business cycles could have complex effects on the demand for and production of export commodities. The supply of necessary inputs might be interrupted, or shipping disrupted; or export prices might fall. The "solution," while not wholly formulated in the 1930s and 1940s, represented a departure from orthodoxy. Recovering from international depression required leaving the gold standard. Insulating a country's economy from unforeseen changes in external demand required less reliance on trade and foreign investment, greater domestic political autonomy, an alteration in the composition of domestic production, and a set of economic goals that accorded considerable authority to the state as a leading actor.

The specific policy prescriptions that followed from the stance of export pessimism varied widely, but they are frequently summarized by the phrase "import substitution industrialization." The idea of identifying potential markets for domestic production was not a novel one. Light industries such as textiles, brewing, glass making, and tobacco manufacture had lengthy histories in Latin America. In Mexico and Peru, extensive discussion on the desirability of domestic industrialization dated to the early years of the nineteenth century, as did demands for tariff protection. By the middle of the twentieth century, Latin Americans were able to produce a coherent justification for import substitution based on long historical experience and wedded to the emerging field of development economics. As Raúl Prebisch was to emphasize shortly before his death, the emphasis that he and other Latin Americans placed on autonomous development was not just an economic or a political stance, but an intellectual one as well. [See Raúl Prebisch, "Dependence, Development and Interdependence," in Gustav Ranis and T. Paul Schultz, *The State of Development Economics. Progress and Perspectives* (1988)].

The readings that follow examine these ideas from various perspectives. While it is today fashionable to question the inward-looking strategies that export pessimism supported, Angus Maddison demonstrates that rates of growth in Latin America were nevertheless high. Nora Lustig provides a survey of the intellectual origins of structuralist economic thinking and export pessimism.

Rosemary Thorp emphasizes that the consequences of import substitution should not be confused with its initial goals: much that occurred was the result of circumstances rather than clear intent. Gustav Ranis provides a modern economic rationale for import substitution, and asks why policy choices led Latin America toward secondary import substitution rather than to the export promotion that occurred in East Asia.

Unorthodox Policies
But Rapid Growth

ANGUS MADDISON

Angus Maddison, the author of *Brazil and Mexico* (1992), *Dynamic Forces in Capitalist Development* (1991), *Phases of Capitalist Development* (1982), and other studies of the history of national income growth, here surveys Latin America in the period 1913–1950. Stemming from his finding that the growth rate of Latin America during these years averaged 3.5 percent per year, as against 1.9 percent per year for the advanced capitalist countries, Maddison's fundamental message is clearly stated: "Despite faster demographic growth than elsewhere, Latin America made greater progress in improving real per capita income than did the rest of the world in this period."

Despite considerable controversy about why countries with lower levels of national income generally grow more quickly than countries with higher income levels—the so-called convergence question—Maddison suggests that in Latin America, government direction rather than economic liberalism was the key. Following the lead of Carlos Díaz Alejandro, Maddison argues that Latin America developed new policy instruments to combat the Great Depression, and that these instruments, rather than an adherence to liberal orthodoxy, abetted economic recovery. If the period before World War I had witnessed a general openness to trade, investment, and immigration, the years from the Depression onward

Angus Maddison, "Economic and Social Conditions in Latin America, 1913–50," in Miguel Urrutia, ed., *Long-Term Trends in Latin American Economic Development*, pp. 3, 4, 6, 9–14, 17–19, 21–22. Reprinted by permission of Johns Hopkins University Press.

saw the emergence of active, inward-looking policies characterized by export pessimism and import substitution industrialization. In general, by the early 1970s, Latin America was far less open to trade then it had been on the eve of the Great Depression.

Nevertheless, as Maddison points out, inward-looking policies exacted costs of their own. These included overvalued exchange rates, slow employment growth, and increasingly skewed distributions of income. Moreover, the retreat from the international economy meant that Latin America tended to pay for more expensive oil in the 1970s by borrowing rather than by exporting, a process which had become completely unsustainable by the early 1980s, when real interest rates in the world economy rose sharply. The debt crisis of the 1980s, in other words, brought to a close an economic cycle of some 50 years. On the one hand, inward-looking policies undoubtedly produced substantial per capita growth in Latin America. On the other, they contributed to an accumulation of economic distortions that culminated in the Lost Decade of the 1980s, when living standards nearly everywhere fell dramatically.

The Pre–World War I Years

Before World War I the major countries of Latin America were already incorporated into the growth processes set in motion by the liberal world order of market capitalism. Foremost among these processes was foreign trade. For the nine countries considered in this chapter (Argentina, Brazil, Chile, Colombia, Cuba, Mexico, Peru, Uruguay, and Venezuela), per capita exports averaged $32 in 1913, compared with less than $1 for China and $2.60 for India. Average export levels were in fact not far below those of such major industrialized countries as France and Germany, although Latin American exports were represented largely by a few primary products (see Table 1). Little trade existed among the Latin American countries themselves; most of it was with the developed world, in particular with the United States and the United Kingdom (see Table 2).

Foreign investment was also substantial. By 1914 the cumulative total in both Brazil and Mexico was bigger than each country's gross domestic product (GDP), a relationship that has never since been equaled. In per capita terms, foreign assets in Latin America were probably ten times higher than in the Asian countries. Foreign capital not only provided general finance for government but also financed an infrastructure of ports, electricity, telephones, tele-

Table 1.   Commodity Composition of Latin American Exports, 1929
            (Percentages of total)

Argentina	wheat 29.2; maize 17.6; frozen, chilled, and tinned meat 12.8; linseed oil 12.6
Brazil	coffee 71.0
Chile	nitrates 42.1; copper 40.4
Colombia	coffee 60.6; petroleum 21.3
Cuba	sugar 79.5
Mexico	silver 20.6; other minerals 47.0
Peru	oil 29.7; copper 22.4; wool 21.0; sugar 11.5; lead 5.1
Uruguay	wool 30.7; frozen, chilled, and tinned meat 30.2; hides and skins 12.7
Venezuela	oil 74.2; coffee 17.2

SOURCE: *Statistisches Reichsamt* (1936)

graphs, and railways, particularly in Argentina, Chile, Cuba, Mexico, Uruguay, and southern Brazil.

Latin America also benefited from large-scale immigration, especially from southern Europe, Between 1880 and 1930, Argentina received almost 6 million immigrants and southern Brazil nearly 4 million. The flow was also important for Chile, Cuba, and Uruguay. In the Southern Cone countries, many immigrants were seasonal workers. Nevertheless, they made a substantial contribution to those economies.

A marked difference existed between the level of real income in the advanced capitalist countries and the level in most of the Latin American countries, despite the latter's involvement in world trade. Only in Argentina and Uruguay did real income even approach the European level, and among the remaining countries, Chile was the only one with a per capita income in 1913 significantly higher than that of Japan (see Table 3).

By 1913, most Latin American countries had been politically independent for a century, unlike the African and Asian countries. As a result, a significant number of the Latin American governments were able to exercise greater freedom than the African and Asian governments in pursuing their own national economic interests. Latin American states were less constrained by the "imperialism of

Table 2.   *Geographic Distribution of Latin American Exports, 1929*
(Percentages of total)

	France	Germany	U.K.	U.S.
Argentina	7.1	10.0	32.2	9.8
Brazil	11.1	8.8	6.5	42.2
Chile	6.1	8.6	13.3	25.4
Colombia	0.5	2.1	4.7	75.2
Cuba	2.1	0.8	12.6	76.6
Mexico	3.9	7.6	10.3	60.7
Peru	1.3	6.1	18.3	33.3
Uruguay	11.9	14.5	23.0	11.9
Venezuela	2.9	4.7	1.9	28.2
Average	4.2	7.0	13.6	40.4

SOURCE: *Statistisches Reichsamt* (1936)

free trade" or by the more direct forms of foreign interference that the colonized world of Africa and Asia had to endure. In this respect, within Latin America, countries like Argentina, Brazil, Chile, and Uruguay clearly enjoyed much greater freedom of action than did Cuba, which was virtually a U.S. colony, or Mexico, where foreign economic interests had tremendous influence on government.

Most Latin American countries were free to formulate their own fiscal, monetary, banking, tariff, exchange rate, and commodity stabilization policies, unlike most of the rest of the Third World. Furthermore, the Latin American countries were more given to defying the established wisdom of the gold standard era than were some European countries. In this respect, the country that exercised the greatest autonomy in policy was Brazil, which for decades had had a floating exchange rate and the highest tariffs and largest industrial sector in Latin America, as well as schemes for fostering immigration and supporting the price of coffee . . . .

World War I

World War I constituted a significant external break in the liberal world order—a break that adversely affected export markets, import availabilities, capital flows, migration, and the world price cli-

Table 3.   *Selected Countries' Real Per Capita GDP at Factor Cost,*
1913–1985 (Dollars at 1965 factor cost)

	1913	1929	1938	1950	1980	1985
Argentina	790	908	847	1,037	1,715	1,417
Brazil	118	175	219	310	1,156	1,114
Chile	381	580	556	707	1,116	1,137
Colombia	188	236	265	309	636	637
Mexico	241	252	257	341	904	875
Peru	115	177	194	269	499	432
Venezuela			428	724	1,476	1,199
Japan	332	485	586	465	3,379	3,952
UK	1,059	1,105	1,259	1,440	2,743	2,974
US	1,358	1,767	1,554	2,411	4,254	4,569
India	173	174	161	155	297	333

SOURCE: Figures for Latin American countries (except Mexico) derived by merging time series with benchmark estimates of GDP levels in A. Maddison, *Economic Progress and Policy in Developing Countries* (New York: Norton, 1970), p. 29 with upward adjustment for revision of official 1965 GDP estimate from $618,600 million to $642,609 million. Figures for other countries derived in same manner from time series in A. Maddison, *Journal of Economic Literature*, June 1987, and Maddison, "Alternative Estimates of the Real Product of India, 1900–1946," *Indian Economic and Social History Review*, 1985. Mexican figures are based on a bilateral comparison with Brazil in A. Maddison, *Poverty, Equity and Growth in Brazil and Mexico* (Washington D.C. World Bank.)

mate. But the consequences of this break were probably felt less in Latin America than in the rest of the world economy. Meanwhile, the major internal disruption in the region consisted of the ten years of revolution in Mexico from 1910 to 1920.

Changes in world power relations resulting from the weakening of Europe and the relative strengthening of the United States had some impact on the sources of capital, but the 1920s were basically a reconstructed version of the pre-1913 international economic order. Trade was subject to slightly higher tariffs, but quantitative restrictions and exchange controls were not applied, and the gold standard was reestablished. The big break in the liberal world order was caused by the 1929–1932 crisis, which brought about a collapse in world trade and capital markets and induced major new restrictions on migration, trade, and payments.

The Crash of 1929

The world depression had several negative effects with special impact upon Latin America. The first was a decline in the volume of demand for primary export products. The second was the related decline in the relative prices of primary exports with respect to manufacturing imports. The third was the sudden cessation of the capital flow from Europe and the United States to developing countries. The fourth was the general fall in the world price level, which raised the real burden of debt service. All these effects were felt quite severely in Latin America, because of the region's great openness to the world economy and its heavy trade dependence on the United States, which was at the epicenter of the depression. As a result, Latin America had to cut its import volume by 60 percent between 1929 and 1932. Hence, the 1929–1932 crisis had a greater impact on Latin America than World War I. The crisis broke a pattern of regional integration into the world economy that had lasted for decades and brought with it a new arsenal of economic policy weapons.

The initial regional response to the depression was adherence to old policy weapons and gold standard rules—that is, defense of the exchange rate by tighter monetary and fiscal policy and loss of reserves. Because of the magnitude of the external shock, however, this course was abandoned, and new policy weapons had to be used. Argentina and Uruguay went off the gold standard in 1929, and Brazil and Venezuela soon followed suit, as did Chile, Colombia, Peru, and Mexico two years later. Cuba, whose currency was tied to the U.S. dollar throughout the period, had the least scope for innovative action of all the nine Latin American countries under consideration here.

The new weapons were the exchange controls, quantitative restrictions, and bilateral trade restrictions devised by Dr. Hjalmar Schacht at the Reichsbank in Germany. Tariffs were also increased in response to the general trend, which the United States had initiated with the Smoot-Hawley legislation. Debt delinquency, a weapon that had been used by individual countries at different times in the past, was almost universal; the old mechanisms of renegotiation were used, although the ultimate outcome was much larger write-offs than in the past (except for Argentina).

New regional blocs came into being in the British, Dutch, French, and Japanese empires, but not in Latin America. Cuba, which was virtually a U.S. colony, was actually shut out of the preferential sugar-marketing arrangements the United States created for the Philippines and Puerto Rico. Argentina did continue to have access to the United Kingdom's market, but only because of the Roca-Runciman agreement, which prevented Argentina from using the weapon of debt delinquency.

The 1930s

Economic recovery in the 1930s was aided by abandonment of an orthodoxy that would have required deflationary action to achieve a balanced budget and to service the foreign debt. As is clear from the recollections of Prebisch, the new policy that was cobbled together was not inspired by any particular new ideology or theory but was instead a muddled and stumbling reaction to new challenges. It was not derived from any theoretical insight but reflected elements common to Latin American countries, such as rejection of the old liberal economic order, a switch to government intervention, and nationalist autarkic measures laced with a dash of populism. These new policies obviously entailed some waste and error. Even so, Latin America's mistakes in policy were generally much less pronounced than those of the United States; Latin American institutional arrangements stood up better, and there was no parallel in the region to the collapse of the U.S. banking system.

Debt delinquency was a vital element in this policy mix. Lewis reported that by the end of 1935 there was 100 percent delinquency on dollar debt by Chile, Colombia, Mexico, Peru, Uruguay, and Venezuela; 93 percent by Brazil; 63 percent by Cuba; and 24 percent by Argentina (by municipalities and provinces, not by central government). This delinquency gained legitimacy because of the concurrent defaults on war debts and reparations payments by the major European countries, and it provided very substantial balance of payments relief. One of its consequences was a rather long period of low foreign investment in Latin America; nevertheless, investment did not disappear completely and reemerged on a large scale in the 1960s and 1970s.

In general, monetary policy was accommodating and helped finance budget deficits worsened by the shortfall in government revenues from import and export duties. With the help of Kemmerer and Niemeyer, central banks had been set up in the 1920s as an independent brake on expansionary government policies. These banks did not function as originally intended, however, after the abandonment of the gold standard. Instead, the banks, or the corresponding monetary authorities generally accommodated sectors of the economy that were in difficulty. . . .

Budgetary policy was also accommodating, but finance ministers were obliged to find new sources of tax revenue. In the 1920s, about half of government revenue in Brazil and more than 60 percent in Colombia had been derived from duties on foreign trade. During the crisis, income and corporate taxes had to be introduced, and excise duties on domestic production had to be raised in order to fill the budget gap. As a result, the tax structure changed considerably.

In general terms, an accommodating policy maintained the overall stimulus to expansion, while specific incentives to industrial production were provided by the increased relative cost of imports and by quantitative restrictions on their entry. These two factors gave a significant boost both to import-substituting industrialization, which was backed by government credit facilities, and to the gradual creation of development banks, whose managers could influence the direction of subsidized credit in line with increasingly specific government policies on the type of production the state wished to encourage.

World War II and the Postwar Years

From the vantage point of 1950, the Latin American countries had considerable reason for satisfaction with their past economic achievements. All the countries except Colombia had been deeply affected by the 1929–1932 crisis but had made a strong recovery that continued through the World War II years. Despite supply shortages, the countries had been able to grow successfully and to achieve rather easy import substitution without a large switch of resources to capital formation or any massive effort at universal education (although some countries strengthened vocational training along German lines—particularly Brazil and Colombia). The average GDP growth for Latin America for the 1913–1950 period was 3.5 percent per year as against only 1.9 percent per year for the advanced capitalist countries and as against much less than 1.9 percent for the big countries of Asia. Despite faster demographic growth than elsewhere, Latin America made greater progress in improving real per capita income than did the rest of the world in this period. In the postwar years, the European countries had to be given large-scale U.S. aid under the Marshall Plan, but Latin America's growth was bolstered by improved terms of trade and wartime reserve accumulations and escaped the bottlenecks that war damage inflicted on the European and Asian countries. The difference in economic experiences, particularly from 1929 to 1950, was probably the major reason for postwar policy differences between Latin American countries and member countries of the Organization for Economic Cooperation and Development (OECD).

After World War II, productivity in the economies of Europe was greatly hampered by trade controls, currency restrictions, and other barriers to international commerce. One of the conditions for Marshall aid on which the liberally oriented U.S. administration insisted was the removal of these barriers and the creation of a neoliberal order encompassing free trade, free migration, and unrestricted capital movements. Until 1971 this policy was buttressed by the Bretton Woods fixed exchange rate system and by the creation of the OECD as a forum for government consultations on economic policy. Many Europeans were highly skeptical about this liberalism at the time, but the combination of U.S. aid and the Stalinist threat greatly strengthened the policy's credentials.

In fact, this new type of managed economic liberalism had many favorable direct and indirect effects on economic growth in Europe and also influenced the character of policy in other domains. The openness of the economies reduced the scope for detailed planning and *dirigisme* and forced European governments to follow reasonably balanced fiscal and monetary policies in order to maintain external equilibrium, while the fixed exchange rate expectation affected the climate of wage bargaining and entrepreneurial price setting. Competition from foreign trade helped to mitigate price rises in Europe.

In Latin America, there was no parallel reversion to international or domestic economic liberalism in the 1950s and 1960s, even though most countries of the region did join the International Monetary Fund (IMF) and the General Agreement on Tariffs and Trade (GATT). There was no Marshall aid or Stalinist threat in the region, the immediate shortages of commodities and of liquidity were smaller than in Europe, and the economies of the region had never been as highly integrated as those of Europe. The region's growth experience of the 1930s and during World War II had been relatively favorable, so inward-looking protectionist policies did not lose their appeal.

In an influential report to the new Economic Commission for Latin America (ECLA), Raúl Prebisch was extremely pessimistic about the outlook for trade as an engine of growth and asserted that in any case a liberal world order had an inherent bias against the welfare of so-called peripheral countries because liberalism brought about a steady long-term reduction in peripheral countries' terms of trade. Prebisch and the ECLA Secretariat gradually built a development theory around the inward-looking assumption and around the idea that the policy tasks of governments in the developing countries were different from those in developed countries—particularly in regard to the need for structural change. They endorsed most of the dirigiste apparatus created in the 1930s, and the momentum of politics also pointed in the direction of continuity and a rejection of both the old and the new tenets of liberalism. The influence of such policies is clear: the steady closing of Latin American countries to international trade compared with the increased openness of the OECD countries. In the 1970s, Latin American policy attitudes did eventually change to give greater emphasis to export promotion and to diversification toward manufactures. Some success was attained in both areas, but the efforts to build up intraregional trade in the Latin American Free Trade Association (LAFTA), the Andean Pact (ANCOM), and the Central American Common Market (CACM) had only limited success. . . .

The 1970s

The depth of the general difference in economic policy attitudes between Latin America and the OECD countries became even clearer after the first oil shock (1974), which created problems of inflation and payments equilibrium throughout the world economy. Inflation in European countries and in the United States reached levels that reactivated old orthodoxies and caution; inflation control quickly became the major aim of policy there, even at a substantial cost to growth and employment. Thus there occurred a very sharp and general cutback in growth in the OECD countries from 1973 to 1980.

In Latin America also, some changes took place in policy emphasis and weaponry, particularly in the Southern Cone countries (Argentina, Chile, and Uruguay), where military regimes experimented with neoconservative radicalism. But generally, Latin America used the very large possibilities for foreign borrowing in the

1970s to continue to give primary emphasis to developmental objectives. This developmentalist policy did not seem overly risky at the time, because interest rates were substantially negative, growth rates were a good deal higher from 1973 to 1980 than in the OECD countries, and inflation was considered merely a nuisance rather than a bogey.

The 1980s and Early 1990s

Following the 1980 oil shock, the situation in Latin America changed completely. Most countries had major recessions, GDP growth was slower than in the 1930s, and adjustment problems were different from (and in some ways more difficult to solve than) those in the 1930s. Inflation reached intolerable levels, and the inertia and disequilibria in public finance were powerful enough to defeat virtually all the desperate remedies applied. In the post-Crash 1930s, the problems of intractable inflation had not existed; such inflation was clearly the outcome of events in subsequent decades. Furthermore, the debt problem of the 1980s was different from that of the 1930s; the bulk of debt in the 1980s was governmental debt to well-organized foreign banks at historically very high interest rates; in the 1930s debt delinquency had been achieved more quickly and completely, with less negotiation and much greater balance of payments relief. But as of the early 1990s, the simple option of regional withdrawal from the world economy by easy import substitution, which was followed in the 1930s, is neither sensible nor possible. It is not sensible in that world trade volumes and prices have not collapsed as they did in the 1930s. It is not possible in that it has already been tried unsuccessfully; such an option has been largely exhausted by past policy, which has reduced the openness of the Latin American economies without achieving lasting economic benefits for the region.

Some of the present problems of Latin America have clearly been created by external circumstances, particularly the OECD countries' policy stance after the second oil shock, a stance that involved very tough monetary and (except in the United States) fiscal measures. Such domestic economic policies cut the pace of those countries' local inflation drastically but raised world interest rates and cut the pace of economic growth well below its potential, thereby helping to induce the Latin American debt crisis and accentuating the contrasts in economic policy objectives in different parts of the world economy. Other current regional economic problems, however, have been generated by Latin America itself. Even if all its foreign debt were written off, the region would still face major difficulties in getting onto a path of "stabilizing development," or *desarrollo estabilizador.*

Import Substitution: A Good Idea in Principle

ROSEMARY THORP

Rosemary Thorp is the author of *Peru, 1890–1977: Growth and Policy in an Open Economy* (with Geoffrey Bertram, 1978), *Latin American Debt and the Adjustment Crisis* (1987), and *Economic Management and Economic Development in Peru and Colombia* (1991). Here Thorp considers the origins of import substitution industrialization in some detail. Although Stephen Haber suggests that industry in Latin America did not inevitably prosper because of the Great Depression, Thorp argues that economic recovery in the region was centered around exports, because of currency devaluation, improvements in international prices, and policy support. During World War II, export growth complemented the economic stimulus that import substitution provided. But this sort of balance was generally not maintained after World War II.

Flush with revenues from wartime sales, Latin American countries had little incentive to maintain realistic exchange rates as domestic prices rose. Moreover, the failure of Latin America to gain aid analogous to the Marshall Plan from the United States after the war made the liberal trade regime that the United States advocated unattractive. As a result, the capital that flowed into the region supported industries "in a context of . . . actual levels of protection . . . far higher than ever dreamed of by the theorists of [import substitution]." In short, Thorp concludes that the weaknesses of the import substitution model were not intrinsic to it, but devel-

Rosemary Thorp, "A Reappraisal of the Origins of Import-Subsisting Industrialization, 1930–1950," *Journal of Latin American Studies,* 24: Quincentenary Supplement (1992) pp. 181–182, 184–187, 188–189, 195. Reprinted by permission of Cambridge University Press.

oped as a result of complex international circumstances following World War II. Thinking about "development from within" (*desarollo desde adentro*) had become "inward-looking development" (*desarollo hacia adentro*). Latin America's retreat from the international economy after World War II was unplanned.

The current enthusiasm for trade liberalization in Latin America, and indeed for a broad-ranging return to the market, has as its backdrop the widespread disillusion with the protectionist model of the 1950s and 1960s. Import substituting industrialisation (ISI) is seen as having used tariff barriers and controls to generate an extremely inefficient industry, suffering under a weight of state bureaucracy, with often inappropriate direct state participation. Its excessive import needs, for all its import-substituting origin, are directly related to the generation of the debt crisis. The high and poorly structured tariffs brought tariff-hopping foreign investment on inappropriate terms. Repressed domestic interest rates allowed such firms to borrow locally at negative real rates and crowd out locals who then borrowed abroad. This inefficiency, plus the overvalued exchange rates implicit in heavy protection, made exports of manufactures unthinkable, and thus condemned the incipient industry to severe limitations of market size as well as condemning the economies to growing balance of payments non-viability. This in turn severely affected industrial progress by limiting growth and exposing firms to stop-go policies.

In turn, ISI policies themselves are seen as having originated with the turning point of the 1929 depression, when the export-led growth mechanism essentially broke down and at least the more sizeable Latin American economies turned fatally inwards. The trajectory from 1930 to the 'fully-fledged' ISI model of the 1950s and 1960s is typically left vague.

This article will attempt to show that recent research now allows us a much fuller and more nuanced view of the evolution from the export economy model of the early century through to the later ISI model. In telling the story in some detail, we are able to teach conclusions concerning the initial potential of the model, the circumstances which made the early version a promising and reasonable route, and the factors which led to its subsequent distortion and heavily negative characteristics. . . .

A significant piece of recent research by Bulmer-Thomas explores the sources of growth in the 1930s, using the Chenery categories (proportions due to exports, home demand from various sources, and import substitution). He is able to show that the contribution of import substitution is negative in a technical sense for the period 1932–9, despite its leading role in the early years (1928–32) in response to shortages. What makes this possible is the recovery in exports. The latter is a function of several things. The net barter terms of trade recovered between 1933 and 1937, based as much on weakness of import prices as on export price recovery. By 1939, for all Latin America the net barter terms of trade had recovered to their 1930 level, and were 36% above the 1933 level. Stronger forces in most cases were volume increases responding partially to international events and partially to internal policy. Key policy measures, coupled with export growth, contributed to the recovery in internal demand: politically, it was essential to support the export sector and this required, first, spending, and second, various kinds of debt alleviation. In the spending category comes Brazil's buying up of coffee and Colombia's completion of vital infrastructure projects for the coffee sector. Debt alleviation occurred in many countries, becoming widespread as debt default also became a public sector necessity. (As countries moved off the gold standard and exchange rates depreciated, debt service burdens rose to impossible levels as a percentage of government revenue—often 70%.) By 1933, only Argentina, Honduras, Haiti and the Dominican Republic had not defaulted. (Venezuela did not need to, having already paid off its debt.) Colombia continued to service central government debt until 1934.

Policies, however, also went further and considerable real devaluation occurred in the course of the decade. In Brazil, for example, exporters enjoyed a 49% real devaluation based on the official exchange rate, and an 80% real depreciation based on the free market rate. This was possible, of course, because the link between depreciation of the exchange rate and internal inflation was still weak. In the first years, internal prices were falling faster than abroad and this produced the real depreciation. Subsequently, prices began to rise moderately, but with much excess capacity and lack of inflationary expectations, there was no sign yet of the pernicious inflationary features of the 1970s and 1980s.

Defence of the balance of payments certainly also led to increases in tariffs and the use of direct controls, but the substantial shift of relative prices in favour of import-competing activity was achieved as much by devaluation, with multiple exchange rates, as by tariffs. The result was that the export sector recovered and flourished alongside the rapid expansion of the industrial sector. At least for the time being, the major Latin American countries had found that delicate balance whereby they could diversify without killing the goose that laid the golden eggs — the export sector.

There are two significant exceptions to the export story: Argentina and Mexico. If we exclude these two from the data on Latin America, the volume of the remaining 18 rose by 53% between 1932 and 1939. The poor performance of Mexico is easy to explain, since exports in fact grew rapidly from 1932 to 1937, only to collapse in the wake of oil nationalisation in 1938. The case of Argentina has been the subject of much analysis. It was a product both of dependence on the British market and of real exchange rate movements.

The positive role of primary exports and the support they received from policy is no surprise, given the data we presented at the start of this section. With the significant exception of Argentina, even our five largest economies were still heavily trade dependent in the 1930s, with relatively small industrial sectors. Since Argentina was the one exception where the export sector was not favoured, the exception is consistent with the case we are making for trade dependence inhibiting discrimination against the primary export sector. The situation in relation to trade dependence changed, however, even in the course of the decade. By the following decade, as we now go on to show, the situation became more fluid.

In one sense, the war [the Second World War] actually allowed the continuation of the special mix which we are identifying as healthy for the evolution of ISI, for Latin America became an important source of raw materials, and thus experienced even stronger growth of exports, while at the same time the difficulty of import supply created an independent stimulus to continued import substitution. Not only was industry able to grow rather fast, if unevenly, but also the process acquired for the first time a regional dimension, as trade in manufactures opened up between Latin American countries.

The country experience with exports naturally varied widely, but practically every country experienced export growth at constant prices of over 4% a year. However, a country's ability to benefit from this varied widely, as for example in the case of minerals, price controls and delayed payments meant little extra revenue received. This explains the relatively limited growth of export revenues of mineral exporters such as Chile, Bolivia and Peru. But even where revenues were available there was little to spend them on: there was thus substantial accumulation of reserves, although again to a variable extent, and contradictory forces operated on industry. Scarcity of imports certainly encouraged new efforts at substitution, but these same efforts were limited in turn by scarcity of crucial imports and machines. The net result was a continuation of the industrial growth already experienced during the 1930s, but with a new bias towards capital goods and basic inputs. For example, a number of the firms later to be important in the Brazilian capital goods industry evolved from the workshop to factory in this period. . . .

In the years following the war, two models were in play to guide the ISI process. The first view responded to US interests and to more conservative interests within Latin America, and wanted a radical reversion to market forces with low protection and an open door for foreign private capital. The second view was that beginning to emerge under the auspices of the recently formed United Nations, Economic Commission for Latin America (ECLA). This view wanted state-induced industrialisation, using modest and efficiently managed protection to overcome market failure, and relying on inflows of public foreign money to ease bottlenecks and facilitate the process. At the core of this approach was an analysis of why Latin American economies would not respond 'automatically' to the price signal of the terms of trade: the reason was 'structural rigidities'— market imperfections rooted in infrastructural deficiencies and in institutions and social and political systems and values. The economies therefore required deliberate government promotion of industrialisation. Foreign capital inflows were helpful to ease the overcoming of rigidities, but the ECLA of the 1950s envisaged such inflows as coming in the form of public sector money. Autonomy was definitely an issue, but industrialisation was to be the answer, providing independence from unstable and undynamic primary exports. No contradiction was seen in using foreign money to achieve this, channelled through government, and issues such as external constraints on policy options were not directly tackled.

Although the internal market was important in this view, the model was not exclusively inward-looking. Temporary protection would lead to new exports, and much emphasis was placed in the early documents on endogenous sources of productivity growth to make this possible in a way compatible with autonomy and long-run comparative advantage. The phrase 'desarrollo *desde* adentro' occurs in Prebisch's early writing, in contrast to the later description of reality 'desarrollo *hacia* adentro', and expresses the idea that the Latin American economies should be integrated to the international economy, but in a way that reinforced internal capacities, respected autonomy and built up long-run comparative advantage.

This view was based on a realistic assessment of the imperfections of the market and on a healthy concept of dynamic comparative advantage, but on a somewhat naïve confidence in the capacity and coherence of the public sector and on loans being available from abroad in a form that would not distort resource allocation. . . .

This article has attempted to fill out the transition from the outward-oriented model of the early years of the century to the ISI model in full swing in the 1950s and 1960s. It has attempted to show that the many negative features of the final model were not intrinsic to it, and certainly not intended by its early theorists, who wanted a moderately protectionist model with heavy emphasis on efficiency and technical progress and a limited role for direct foreign investment [DFI] within that. Their concept, we have argued, was closer to 'desarrollo *desde* adentro' than to the version which in fact developed, which was without doubt, and disastrously, 'desarrollo *hacia* adentro'. The paper has emphasised the early success of the policies in the 1930s, and has shown how far that was due to finding an elusive combination — diversification of the economy and at the same time protection and even stimulation of what was still the life blood of the system: foreign exchange coming from primary exports. We have emphasised the role of the unfortunate combination of events during the Second World War, which left Latin America with exceptionally overvalued exchange rates, accumulated reserves, and inflationary pressures from both internal and external sources. In addition, in the 1940s traditional export markets mostly brought rapidly rising revenues. All this led to policy decisions which cumulatively made it inconceivable that policy makers could have stepped back and opted for a realignment of exchange rates. The 'elusive combination' became very unlikely, just as the political weight of the traditional export sectors began to be diminished. Of our five sizeable economies, only in Colombia did the exceptional weight and degree of organisation of the coffee sector successfully maintain some counterbalancing force to moderate the extreme distortions of ISI. We have also emphasised that the protectionist moves of the 1940s were encouraged by the failure of Latin American overtures to the international system. Furthermore, as public money did not materialise, it became only too likely that country after country would begin to move in the direction of strong incentives to DFI, yet in the context of underdeveloped planning and regulatory machinery which meant that the resulting wave of DFI was essentially unregulated and unmonitored. Again, the distinctive features of the partial exception—Colombia—underline the importance of the political economy characteristics leading to this answer.

Structuralism and Other "Heresies"

NORA LUSTIG

Nora Lustig is the editor or author of a number of important studies, including *North American Free Trade: Assessing the Impact* (1992) and *Mexico: The Remaking of an Economy* (1992). In the article excerpted here, Lustig examines the origins and transformation of the structuralist current of economic thinking in Latin America. In the 1950s, the Economic Commission for Latin America (ECLA), under the leadership of the Argentine economist Raúl Prebisch, attempted to explain the sources of Latin America's unsatisfactory economic performance. Persistent problems with the balance of payments and declining terms of trade reduced both employment and growth in national income. In the broadest sense, these problems reflected different kinds of specialization in the developed and underdeveloped economies. In Latin America, specialization in the production and export of primary commodities concentrated income and wealth in the hands of landowning elites and left the economies subject to considerable instability in prices and income. Typical patterns of consumption offered little hope

Nora Lustig, "From Structuralism to Neostructuralism: The Search for a Heterodox Paradigm," in Patricio Meller, ed., *The Latin American Development Debate. Neostructuralism, Neomonetarism, and Adjustment Processes* (Boulder, CO: Westview Press), pp. 27–31, 34–35, 37–39. Reprinted by permission of Patricio Meller.

that the difficulties would lessen over time. In the developed economies, on the other hand, the production of manufactured goods for export at increasingly favorable relative prices was associated with increased savings and investment and the development of powerful urban interest groups whose political demands were an important element in the creation of liberal democracies. The logic of Prebisch's analysis, coupled with the disruption of international trade during the Great Depression and World War II, acted as a powerful agent in legitimating state-directed industrialization.

In this brief survey of the history of structuralist thought, Nora Lustig explores the complex and sometimes contrary notions that the term *structuralism* implies. She considers the intellectual roots of structuralism and its early evolution in the 1950s. She then passes to structural pessimism in the 1960s, with its emphasis on the persistence of income inequality and balance-of-payments difficulties. She closes with a consideration of neostructuralism in the 1980s, which acted as an intellectual justification for heterodox stabilization policies in the 1980s, as well as for the successful incomes policy followed in Mexico until the unfolding of the crisis of 1994–1995.

Among the numerous intellectual efforts undertaken by Latin American authors to understand the economic phenomena of the region, the current of thought known as *stucturalism* stands out for its originality and persistence. Although structuralist ideas have sometimes been incomplete or unrigorous, over the years they have enriched our comprehension of certain economic processes in the region and suggested fruitful alternative approaches for policy design.

In what follows I shall outline the theoretical roots and summarize the historical evolution of structuralist thought from its inception at the end of the 1940s to the more recent emergence of what is called *neostructuralism*. Although this chapter reveals some of the shortcomings and qualities of structuralist ideas, it does not assess the analytical and empirical validity of structuralism either by itself of vis-à-vis alternative theories.

The Theoretical Roots of Structuralism

At the risk of sounding redundant, one can start by saying that structuralist thought views *structural* characteristics as the basic determinants of a society's evolution. These structural factors include, for example, the distribution of wealth and income, the land tenure regimes, the type and degree of foreign trade specialization, the density of productive linkages, the degree of market concentration, the control of the means of production by different types of actors (i.e., the private sector, the state, and transnational capital), the functioning of financial mechanisms, and the penetration of technological innovation, as well as the sociopolitical factors associated with the degree of labor organization, the organization of other classes or influential sectors, and the geographic and sectorial distribution of the population and its skill level. In structuralism, these characteristics determine the specific functioning of the causal mechanisms and the predictable success of any development strategy.

Structuralist thought—either in its most radical form associated with the Marxist tradition, or in its reformist version linked to the Keynesian and institutionalist schools of thought—falls within the realm of political economy. In the structuralist framework, the conception of society as the sum of family units and atomized firms that face given economic parameters has no meaning. On the contrary, economic policy measures are thought to affect the behavior of social actors who, far from functioning as isolated individuals, tend to join together and generate pressure groups (on either an organized or a spontaneous basis).

The classical roots of structuralist thought can be traced back to the Schumpeterian/Marxist view of free-enterprise capitalism as an inherently conflictive rather than harmonious system, and to its development as an irregular series of jumps that generate countless other imbalances. Although no version of the theory of exploitation appears explicitly in any of the structuralist literature, the notions of surplus generation and appropriation do emerge—along with identification of the losers in this process: the periphery versus the center, workers versus capitalists, campesinos versus the urban sector, and, finally, the very poor versus the rest of society. Nonetheless, the main difference between structuralist and Marxist thought is that structuralist authors do not necessarily conclude either that capitalism will tend to destroy itself or that encouragement of its destruction is necessarily convenient or desirable.

The theoretical precursors of structuralism are various. As I mentioned earlier, the most evident ties are with the Marxist/Schumpeterian tradition, with respect to the vision of the functioning of the whole system. At the level of the specific mechanisms determining prices and product, the link is clearly with the Keynesian and post-Keynesian theories, with Kalecki, and, more recently, with the analytical developments of neo–Ricardian thought. Thus, one can identify some of the assumptions that structuralist analyses have in common. The most important of these are as follows:

1. The most relevant social actors are not price takers; these social actors thus create important rigidities in the markets.
2. The causal relation does not go from savings to investment but, rather, in the opposite direction.
3. In general, the money supply is passive and is adjusted to inflation, not the other way around.
4. Public investment is complementary and encourages private investment.
5. The development process is neither balanced nor harmonious, and it arises from the incorporation and dissemination of technical progress. New investment is the principal instrument in this process.
6. From a technological point of view, imported goods may be fundamental; hence the foreign exchange to purchase them becomes an indispensable requirement for sustained growth.

As a group these assumptions produce what can be called "critical skepticism" toward the recommendations that arise from economic orthodoxy for solving short- and long-term economic problems. In particular, structuralist thought greatly mistrusts the unanimous orthodox recommendation of correctly aligning relative prices as a sufficient (or sometimes even necessary) means of remedying all evils.

This distrust derives from some of the assumptions already mentioned. Due to the intrinsic rigidity of some markets, the adjustments induced by the orthodox recommendations more often change output levels, or income distribution, than prices. Moreover, even if the assumption of price flexibility is accepted, the reallocation of resources that results from the change in prices may not be the best one. For example, partial liberalization in noncompetitive economies does not necessarily lead to a position of greater welfare than that resulting from price intervention. This result has been expanded on and accepted by orthodox welfare theory: The second-best option is not obtained by a partial approach toward the freeing of markets.

Furthermore, even in the case of a competitive world, the alignment of domestic prices with international ones is theoretically not the best policy for long-term growth. It is true that under competitive conditions the correct alignment of prices results in welfare improvement, as measured by static profits. However, it has been demonstrated that, in a dynamic model, a productive specialization different from the one dictated by international prices may result in increased growth over time. Two such circumstances are the presence of increasing economies of scale and uneven technical progress between productive sectors. Such productive specialization can also occur when the price and income elasticities of exports and imports as well as the capacity utilization rate reach certain magnitudes.

Regardless of whether these ideas were developed with the same rigor during the first years of structuralist thought, they were clearly behind Raúl Prebisch's notion of industrial development as the best way to achieve sustained growth. Even if this policy meant a loss of welfare, due to the inefficiencies it introduced over the short term, industrial development was considered to be the most effective way of attracting and instituting dynamic comparative advantages.

The First Stage of Structuralist Thought: The 1950s

It can be said that Latin American structuralist thought officially began at the end of 1949 and the beginning of 1950 with the publication by the Economic Commission for Latin America (ECLA) of two documents: "The Economic Development of Latin America and Some of Its Main Problems" and "The Economic Study of Latin America 1949." In spite of the fact that they are official documents of an organism dependent on the United Nations, the ideas set forth in them can be attributed primarily to one author, Raúl Prebisch.

These papers developed, for the first time, the original concept of the center-peripheral system. According to the analysis presented in them, the capitalist world can be conceptualized as consisting of two types of countries: the center, conformed by those economies in which capitalist production techniques first predominated; and the periphery, which is "constituted by economies whose production continues to lag behind in an organizational and technical point of view," and in which "technical progress only occurs in a few sectors of its enormous population. Generally, it only penetrates those sectors where food and raw materials must be produced at a low cost for large industrial centers."

One of the consequences of this process is that the structure of the periphery acquires two fundamental characteristics. On the one hand, the peripheral economy is specialized, inasmuch as development occurs almost exclusively in the primary-goods export sector whereas other goods and services are usually imported. On the other hand, the peripheral structures are heterogeneous. Those sectors that use advanced techniques imported from the centers, and in which there is a comparable level of labor productivity, coexist with others in which obsolete, old-fashioned techniques are used, thus leading to productivity levels very much inferior to those in analogous activities in the centers.

However, the most important aspect of the central-periphery concept is the idea that these characteristics of the peripheral productive structure, far from disappearing as capitalism advances in the centers, tend to perpetuate and reinforce themselves. One of the determinants of this increasing gap between the two poles is that technological change is much more pronounced in the industrial sector than in the primary sector. Under conditions of constant terms of trade, the former leads to an increase in the productivity and to an income gap between the center and the periphery. This polarization tends to increase given that the centers are able to keep the fruits of technical progress due to the degree of organization of the working class and the oligopolist power of the private business sector. In the periphery, by contrast, productivity increases are not translated into lower prices owing to the structural labor surplus. Furthermore, the income elasticity of raw materials is smaller than that of industrial goods. In other words, there are inherent forces that cause a secular deterioration of the terms of trade, to the continual disadvantage of the periphery.

In view of this interpretation, the development of the periphery has fundamentally depended not on continuing with the historical pattern of specialization based on exploiting static comparative advantages but, instead, on promoting industrial development. Such development can be achieved through import substitution. It can also be achieved if the *infant industries* are furnished with the necessary protection.

The theory of the *deterioration of terms of trade* gave rise to a long theoretical and empirical debate, which experienced various changes later on. Apart from the empirical validity of this theory, the relevance of structuralist thought in its initial stages had to do with the emphasis it placed on the limitations associated with a development pattern based on static comparative advantages. According to the ideas of the period, the productive specialization arising from that pattern would condemn the periphery to remain underdeveloped.

The predominant idea, then, was that development implied industrialization, inasmuch as this was the only course that allowed the peripheral economies to break with the negative characteristics of their productive structure and to make full use of the advantages derived from technical progress. . . .

Structural Pessimism: The 1960s

The relative failure of industrialization via import substitution became evident in three areas: First, the problem of external imbalance became more acute for the reasons referred to already. Second, serious sectoral imbalances appeared. For example, the agricultural sector became less dynamic, resulting in bottlenecks in the production of foodstuffs (and, hence, in inflationary pressures); the use of capital-intensive techniques in industry led to the surfacing of urban impoverishment because industry was unable to absorb quickly enough the labor force that was arriving in the cities in search of a better standard of living; and because more priority was placed on physical goals than on those of efficiency, plants were constructed that would always operate at excess capacity. Finally, as the import-substitution process advanced, the real resources initially transferred to industry by the agro-industrial sector decreased (as a consequence of the stagnation of agricultural production), and the process depended more and more on state intervention and subsidies.

At the same time, public expenditures that were complementary to the industrialization process increased (owing to infrastructure projects, for example, or because the government became the last-resort employer), and the potential growth of government income became restricted. An imbalance in the public finances was thus unleashed, resulting in demand pressures that contributed to the inflationary process.

Disappointment with the results of the import-substitution process gave way to new currents of thought within structuralism. One group placed its hopes on regional integration. During this period several efforts were made to bring about subregional integration; this position continues to be held today among the advoates of south-south commerce as the best option for indebted countries. . . .

The Emergence of Neostructuralism: The 1970s and 1980s

In the time since the positions on growth and income distribution were elaborated, structuralist thought seems to have concentrated more and more on short-term problems and policies. Perhaps this is a natural reaction to the "orthodox" stabilization packages applied in the Southern Cone during the 1960s under the aegis of military regimes. It may also be a response to the difficulties involved in implementing structural change along the lines recommended by the redistributionists, as exemplified by the Chilean case. . . .

In clear contrast with structuralism, in fact, it might be said that neostructuralist thought has the opposite bias: a lot of emphasis on short-term analysis and relatively little emphasis on the long run. The reason for this might be that the short-term problems are so pressing that intellectual energy has been directed toward them rather than toward long-term problems. It may also be that adequate long-term strategies are less clear. The negative consequences of recommendations in the more "naive" version of structuralism (i.e., regarding the efficiency of the public and private productive apparatus) have resulted in more skepticism concerning direct or indirect state intervention in the allocation of resources. Democracy has reappeared in many countries, and the desire to maintain this form of government has made economic policy more cautious. Years of dictatorship and repression are evidence of political fragility and of the sensitivity of many societies to conflictive measures. In neostructuralist thought there is the clear perception that solutions must be reached through consensus.

Finally, the opinion that a viable long-run strategy is impossible under the current conditions of foreign debt servicing seems to make long-term analyses irrelevant until the conditions change. However, the existence of this restriction demonstrates the urgency of finding new formulas that make more equitable growth strategies a viable option. In other words, formulas must be found that permit the original proposals of structuralist thinking to observe real-world examples.

Why Latin America Borrowed
When East Asia Exported

GUSTAV RANIS

Gustav Ranis is the author of *Development of the Labor Surplus Economy* (1964, with John C. H. Fei), *Growth with Equity: the Taiwan Case* (1979, with John C. H. Fei and Shirley W. Y. Kuo), and other major studies. One feature of Ranis's work has addressed an often-remarked difference between the development strategies of East Asia and Latin America. Although such comparisons are inevitably oversimplified, observers often contrast East Asia's export orientation with Latin America's inward-looking import substitution. Small, resource-poor nations such as Taiwan are logical candidates for an outward-looking, export-oriented strategy, given limited domestic markets. But larger, resource-rich countries such as Mexico and Brazil had an incentive to industrialize with substantial protection and to focus more exclusively on sizable internal markets. Geopolitical considerations, domestic class structure, and the strength of the state also figure in analyses of why East Asia's development trajectory diverged from Latin America's. The differences matter. As repeated studies have shown, East Asia enjoys flatter distributions of income, lower levels of foreign indebtedness, and more rapid growth than does Latin America.

Gustav Ranis, "Contrasts in the Political Economy of Development Policy Change," in Gary A. Gereffi and Donald Wyman, eds., *Manufacturing Miracles: Paths of Industrialization in Latin America and East Asia* (Princeton, NJ: Princeton University Press, 1990) pp. 207–208, 220–222, 223–229. Reprinted by permission of Princeton University Press.

In this excerpt, Ranis begins by criticizing the notion that a "unique metamorphic transition growth path" exists. In other words, there is no inevitable or typical pattern of stages of economic growth, as Walt Rostow suggested in his famous book, *The Stages of Economic Growth* (1960). True, Mexico and Brazil, like Taiwan and Korea, shared a common initial reliance on commodity exports (that is, raw materials) between the 1880s and the 1940s. And from the 1930s through about 1960, all four engaged in primary import-substitution—that is, the substitution of domestically produced consumer goods such as food, textiles, clothing, and shoes for their imported counterparts.

Yet such a strategy cannot persist indefinitely. As Ranis puts it, "once all nondurable manufactured goods imports have been substituted . . . any further industrialization has to slow to the pace of population and per capita income change." In other words, once domestic market needs are fully met, what happens next? Does a country seek to export shoes, clothing, and textiles to new markets (called export substitution)? Or does it move into new, more complex lines of manufacturing, such as automobiles, steel, and heavy machinery (termed secondary import substitution)? The evidence suggests that skipping export substitution and moving directly into secondary import substitution involves a substantial cost in *both* equity and efficiency forgone. After World War II, industrializing under protected or artificial conditions meant using price controls or pegged exchange and interest rates to provide resources to well-connected entrepreneurs, or favoring privileged labor groups with substantially higher wages. Fewer jobs were created in industries whose profitability depended on subsidies and a protected domestic market. East Asian industries faced realistic domestic prices, as well as rational interest and exchange rates. As a result, their growth reflected profitability and international demand rather than progressively larger and more costly subsidies, distortions, and transfers.

Since Ranis argues that these differences were not predetermined, but reflected conscious policy choices, he asks, logically enough, why East Asian and Latin American policy choices differed. In the final analysis, he answers that the existence of rich natural resources in Latin America makes the decision to persist in secondary import substitution possible. Industrialization can be funded by agricultural and mineral exports, or by transferring resources from agriculture to industry through price controls that provide cheap food to industrial labor. Resource-poor countries do not have this option, and must instead, as Ranis says, "shift their attention to the deployment of their human resources"—that is, emphasize education and training to raise productivity.

The current interest in comparing East Asia and Latin America, which was not fashionable as little as half a dozen years ago, is based on the acceptance of the notion that different policy choices can, in fact, make a good deal of difference. But the difficulty with most of that literature is that it is largely descriptive in presenting the success of some of the East Asian countries in contrast to the lack of success of some of the Latin American countries. What was accomplished is fully treated, but the basic question of "why" is hardly addressed. Some of the explanation surely resides in differences in such initial conditions as man/land ratios, natural resource endowments, and size. It is much too facile to attribute significant differences in national performance to cultural differences that are not subject to modification by acts of man over time. Confucianism, for example, can hardly be "the" simple answer when we recall the long centuries of stagnation in China.

It is by now well recognized that both the East Asian and Latin American economies did pass through specific subphases of transition growth. First, we encounter the familiar "easy" import substitution subphase focused on nondurable consumer goods. In Latin America this initially occurred in the 1930s as the by-product response to the Great Depression and was continued in the early postwar period as part of a more deliberate, conscious effort to industrialize. The same emphasis on the home production of previously imported nondurable consumer goods can be dated from the early postwar period in the newly independent countries of East Asia.

This so-called easy import substitution in both Latin America and East Asia thus represents the "natural" outgrowth of a prior colonial, agricultural export-focused pattern of resource flows. Once exchange controls are imposed and government intervenes to direct foreign exchange earnings from reinvestment in the traditional export enclaves to these new domestically oriented industrial activities, the patterns in Latin America and East Asia are indeed quite similar. What mainly differentiates the typical East Asian from the typical Latin American economy is the nature of the societal choice made at the inevitable end of this easy import substitution subphase, as domestic markets for nondurables run out. . . .

As we have already pointed out, both the Latin American and East Asian NICS adopted an internally oriented policy during the easy import substitution subphase, deploying macro-policies to provide protection for their new industrial entrepreneurs and insulating them from exogenous disturbances. During this period, monetary, fiscal, and exchange rate policies were used to accommodate deficit finance, permit money creation, and provide windfalls, all to assist private entrepreneurs by manufacturing profits on their behalf. Policy was based on the conviction that interest rates can be artificially repressed to generate profits for this class, and government can acquire all the goods and services it needs by direct action, that is, covert taxation without consent. Price inflation can be depended upon to lighten the repayment burden of entrepreneurs and thus force the public to save. Such direct growth promotion can be undertaken without difficulty as long as the LDC government has the power to monopolize the expansion of the money supply. All it takes is the political will to use its power persistently.

At the end of easy import substitution, when, as we have observed, the policies diverge, we observe a consistent, more or less monotonic, "liberalization process" setting in the East Asian cases, but one beset with oscillation and retrenchment episodes in the Latin American cases. In the realm of monetary policy, this means that the East Asians gradually came to recognize that money should serve principally as a medium of exchange rather than providing the power for government to acquire resources; that the foreign exchange rate should be more realistic; and that the interest rates should approach the cost of capital. This represents a movement toward a relatively greater role for the market and away from the notion that an all-powerful, newly independent government can take care of everything. It also means a shift from "under the table" taxation through inflation to "on the table" taxation with consent, with private entrepreneurs gradually learning to earn more of their profits through competitive productive performance rather than through rent-seeking activities.

This movement, while still more pronounced in East Asia, seems to be gaining ascendancy elsewhere. Viewed in longer run historical perspective, it constitutes an organizational evolution companion to the transition toward the epoch of modern growth—that is, as an economy becomes increasingly complex, sooner or later the notion that economic decisions must be decentralized seems to surface, even in the so-called socialist economies. It should also be recalled that during easy import substitution governments will typically penetrate the market system to determine not only the overall volume of aggregate demand but even individual investment decisions. Such "directional controls" also tend to atrophy as the economy becomes more complex, calling increasingly for market solutions to replace civil servant discretion in determining specific resource allocations.

In contrast with East Asia, this gradual long-term liberalization process has been much less smooth and linear in Latin America, where the existence and persistence of large rents seems to invite the continuation of rent-seeking policies and the return to them at intermittent intervals. It is, moreover, true that the liberalization process may be more disturbed by exogenous shocks in the natural-resource-rich Latin American countries—that is, through price changes in primary products in world markets as well as the business cycle in the industrially advanced countries.

Another specific example is the role of minimum wage legislation, government supported unionism, and other interventions in labor markets, conspicuous by their presence in Latin America and their absence in East Asia. One might, in fact, assert that union unrest and strikes may be an indicator of social unrest traceable (via inflation and income redistribution) to the unevenness for different social groups of the impact of macroeconomic policies. But clearly a differential wage rate structure—that is, much higher real wages for the small urban organized labor force in Latin America—can be extremely damaging to the possibilities of export substitution as the competitive export of labor-intensive manufactured goods can be effectively blocked, contributing to the persistence of unemployment and underemployment.

The major macroeconomic policy instruments—the interest rate, the exchange rate, the change in the money supply, the rate of protection, the rate of taxes, and government expenditures—must all be viewed as tools of the growth-oriented activists in government providing support to certain private sector participants in the mixed economy. The basic principle that underlies such growth promotion is an income transfer strategy, so that the purchasing power generated in the production process, usually by the exploration of raw materials in rural areas, can be transferred, either covertly or overtly, to favored private entrepreneurs or to the government itself. Once notions of liberalization are entertained at the end of easy import sub-stitution, their consideration often begins rather hesitantly because anything smacking of laissez-faire usually runs counter to the linger-ing political ideology that holds that growth is a public concern that must be managed directly by the exercise of political power. Thus both the East Asian and Latin American economies have to contend with the legacy of a prior import substitution phase, which consti-tutes a more or less control-oriented institutional/organizational package even though it may be less severe in the East Asian case.

All the evidence indicates that East Asia more or less pursued a linear path of policy liberalization and registered far and away the best development performance. On the other hand, in Latin Amer-ica we have witnessed a different, less clear-cut and more oscillatory pattern of policy or organizational choices, with market-oriented episodes replaced by a return to import substitution types of inter-vention in a more or less continuously oscillating pattern and ac-companied by much less successful outcomes in terms of any assess-ment of economic performance. . . .

Our fundamental hypothesis is that major policy instruments such as the interest rate, the foreign exchange rate, the rate of pro-tection, the rate of taxation, and the rate of money supply increase must be interpreted as political instruments used by governments to promote growth through the transfer of income among social groups—that is, to manufacture profits for one group at the expense of others. One of the ways to understand the difference between ex-port substitution in East Asia and export promotion plus secondary import substitution in Latin America is to note that the former sys-tems are gradually but consistently shifting away from "under the table," or implicit, income transfers among groups and toward "on the table," or explicit, revenue and expenditure related policies of government. Increasingly, the focus is on taxation, the provision of overheads, and organizational and institutional construction—that is, constituting a more indirect, though by no means less important, role for the government.

The persistence of the import substitution mode (the Latin American path), is related in part to the ability to pay for it—that is, the ample availability of traditional natural resources and, in part, the governments' felt need to try to be viewed as solving all prob-lems, with the possibility of social conflict arising later (e.g., infla-tion with a time lag) put to one side. The best example of this is, of course, the policy of monetary expansion, which may solve a problem of sectoral clashes today but leads to inflation of the typical Latin American type after one or two years. It is in this context that the familiar macro policy tools, including the foreign exchange rate and the interest rate, are interpreted as growth promoting instruments to effect income transfers in the Latin American context. On the other hand, in the East Asian case a continued trend toward liberalization in various markets at the end of primary import substitution is tantamount to the gradual withdrawal of political forces from the economic arena. This can be observed from the comparison of overall tax rates, the relative importance of internal taxes, and the trend of real effective exchange rates.

Let me now schematically contrast the political economy of policy change in the natural-resources-poor East Asian case with the natural-resources-rich Latin American case. First of all, Taiwan's primary import substitution subphase could be relatively mild partly because of its initially strong domestic cohesion, which meant that the government could concentrate on a few basic economic problems and did not have to over-promise and involve itself directly in too many areas simultaneously. Such "mildness" exhibited itself in a relatively high interest rate and anti-inflation policy and an emphasis on closing budgetary deficits in Taiwan as early as the 1950s—a policy that was, moreover, maintained linearly throughout the next three decades. An effort at maintaining realistic exchange rates was adopted by the late 1950s, with quantitative controls and multiple exchange rates abolished by the early sixties. Tariffs, on the other hand, have been maintained at relatively moderate levels until the present day; major tariff reform is currently under way.

In this context it should be recognized that such devices as export processing zones and the rebating of tariffs for exports represented useful transition devices permitting exports to become competitive while the domestic consumer could continue to be "squeezed" through the maintenance of modest tariffs. The political economy significance of these policy devices, also maintained more or less monotonically, is that in the absence of strong vested interests in traditional agricultural exports and its large rents, it became necessary early on to begin to shift toward the export of nontraditional commodities, which encompasses not only the well-known shift from rice and sugar to textiles and electronics but also the prior shift toward such higher valued, labor-intensive agricultural commodities as mushrooms and asparagus. It is also true that the fact that landless farmers were incorporated into new nonagricultural activity more than proportionately—while medium-sized farmers who lost out during the 1949–1951 land reforms became owners of industrial assets through the rent compensation method—diminished the conflict between the two classes early on.

Since liberalization or depoliticization is always difficult, when there is an absence of large rents accruing from agriculture to be allocated to nonagriculture this also means that the struggle for rents in the sectors which have benefited (among the new industrialists) is toned down, that is, the rent-seeking society characteristics are substantially diminished. It should be noted that while there was some pulling and hauling in the late fifties about which path Taiwan should take, necessity sooner or later became the mother of consistent policy change in the direction of depoliticization. When primary import substitution is mild and relatively short-lived, it also means that less fear of foreign competition is built up; hot-house conditions certainly carry the seeds of their own continuation in the political economy sense.

Thus, the role of government quickly shifted from that of implicit intervention through the five major policy instruments—the interest rate, the tariff rate, the exchange rate, the budget deficit, and monetary expansion—to one of a direct role for government in institutional/organizational change. Specifically, this resided increasingly, especially as labor surplus came to an end, in such areas as (1) education, science and technology infrastructure, and patent laws; (2) a second land reform permitting the reconsolidation of small holdings and the transfer of land as well as the appearance of the so-called cultivating firm selling services to farmers; (3) the expansion and reorganization of financial institutions, still under way today, to permit a shift from the public sector's role in directly productive activities, occasioned mainly by the inability to marshal enough private funds for large projects; (4) an early shift from planning for resources to planning for policy coordination; (5) the privatization of public sector activity, which had been postponed to much later in the transition process.

What is interesting about the East Asian case thus is not only the policy changes that were adopted and more or less linearly adhered to but also the sequence in which they were adopted. Developing countries cannot digest all the requisite liberalization moves at the same time—nor does it make sense to do so even if one could. Depoliticization clearly meant, first, a shift from indirect taxation via inflation to taxes—that is, shifting from "under the table" taxes on agriculture to "on the table" taxes. Second, it meant a shift to greater central bank autonomy and an early decline in reliance on the expansion of the money supply accompanied by a higher interest rate policy. Third, a postponement of tariff reductions was forced by the need for revenue, plus the fact that, while foreign consumers could no longer be taken for granted, it was still possible, and necessary, to squeeze domestic consumers for some time to come; meanwhile, export processing zones and tariff rebates for exports were deployed as transitional devices.

Fourth, we might also note that social welfare legislation, including the support of minimum wages and unionism, which really represent acts of government in the sense of helping to share out unearned rents between industrial entrepreneurs and industrial workers, has not been a feature of the East Asian landscape until this day. This phenomenon is often put at the doorstep of a repressive government. However, unless one is unduly mesmerized by the political trappings or legislative protections of an urban working elite it is highly doubtful that the economic participation and welfare of the East Asian populations was adversely affected by such delays in social legislation and unionization. It is indeed also important to better understand the relationship between economic participation and political pluralism.

Let us look at the Latin American natural-resources-rich country type in contrast. Not only does the existence of plentiful natural resources provide the wherewithal for maintaining import substitution longer than would otherwise be desirable, but it also provides the vulnerability to inevitable terms of trade fluctuations. It thus has two effects on the transition growth path. One, it postpones the opening toward competitive exports, in rendering export orientation something that is superimposed "on top of" a continued import substitution structure; second, it means that even when episodes of liberalization are recorded, it makes the system much more vulnerable to backsliding in response to inevitable oscillations in the terms of trade. Thus, what we find in the Latin American case is liberalization/interventionist cycles, as external shocks are felt, around a secular trend of export promotion coupled with continued secondary import substitution as described above.

To be more precise, during a period of terms of trade recovery one might well encounter some liberalization with a devaluation, an increase in the foreign exchange reserves, an increase in the money supply, in tax revenue, and spending. But once the terms of trade deteriorate, one is then likely to encounter a tendency to substitute domestic spending for the decline in foreign exchange reserves. There follow large budget deficits and an increase in the money supply, in combination with an effort to "fix" the exchange rate. The system then gradually drifts back to import substitution type policies, with the exchange rate becoming increasingly overvalued, in order to fight so-called externally caused inflation. Ultimately, a large devaluation does become necessary and the cycle can once again repeat itself.

Thus, what we observe is cycles of retreats to import substitution cum export promotion and shifts back toward liberalization and export substitution in many of the developing countries of Latin America. As a consequence, the shifting of profits from agricultural sources to favored parties in the nonagricultural sector is both maintained for a longer period secularly; and there is always a tendency to drift back toward the import substitution policy syndrome. Both the money supply and the level of exchange reserves are viewed more as instruments for governments' capturing resources rather than as mediums of exchange as they are in the typical developed country.

Thus the seemingly inevitable by-product of a plentiful supply of land-based rents available to a society is a reduced willingness or capacity to withdraw the "goodies" from the major vested interest groups, the urban industrialists and organized labor, and the civil servants who parcel out the specific benefits of import substitution. As a consequence, not only is there much greater hesitation in dismantling quantitative restrictions and tariffs in a secular sense but also unions and minimum wage legislation as a way of sharing out these rents among the privileged groups clearly assume greater importance. Once such legislation does exist and such habits are formed it may well be true that only relatively strong governments can rescind them. In lieu of more taxation with consent, we instead are likely to get more protection, lower real interest rates, more monetary expansion, and more overvalued exchange rates as a way of continuing to manufacture profits for governments and favored interest groups in the nonagricultural sector. It is this broader version of the "Dutch Disease," rather than the narrower impact of natural resource bonanzas on the exchange rate, which has made a large difference in determining the observed differential growth performance as between East Asia and Latin America.

Needless to add, foreign capital inflows "for the asking" can have a similar impact on the political economy of policy change. It is no accident that the current debt crisis, fueled by liberal commercial bank lending in the seventies, has been more pronounced in Latin America than in East Asia. While foreign capital, like natural resources, should theoretically constitute a potential advantage for a system trying to restructure its policies (by enhancing its ability to "bind the wounds" of affected interest groups) the political economy effects are otherwise. The absence of natural resources and the withdrawal of aid are more likely to jolt the system into the realization that it has to rely increasingly heavily on its human resources if it is to navigate successfully in the direction of modern growth.

In sum, when economic rents in the form of returns to nonaugmentable natural resources are predictably scarce and running out, there exists a necessity to depoliticize and liberalize the economy, provide less incentive for various interest groups to do battle for the spoils and thus strengthen the accommodative nature of policy change in the transition growth process. Such countries are then forced by circumstance to shift their attention earlier to the deployment of their human resources, both unskilled and skilled. In Latin America, with less necessity to make such politically difficult decisions, they could more easily be delayed. As a consequence, a good natural resources base and good foreign friends willing to provide foreign capital—both potentially of benefit to a society in soothing the inevitable pains of policy change—are likely to become political economy obstacles to effecting those very changes.

PART V

From Crisis to Crisis: Neoliberalism and Its Discontents

In Latin America and in much of the developing world, the 1980s were known as the Lost Decade. The phrase refers to the substantial reduction in growth that occurred with the onset of the debt crisis in 1982. For example, the growth of per capita income in Latin America in the 1970s averaged 3.3 percent per year. In the 1980s, per capita income fell 1.1 percent yearly as production shrank. In some countries, the decline was severe. Brazil, for instance, had grown at 3.6 percent per capita per year in the 1970s. Income fell 0.7 percent per year in the 1980s. Per capita income in Argentina grew at 0.9 percent per year in the 1970s, but fell at 2.2 percent in the 1980s. Per capita income in Mexico grew at 3.7 percent in the 1970s, but fell by 0.7 percent per year in the 1980s. By the early 1990s, neither Mexico nor Brazil had resumed its growth rate of the 1970s.

During the 1970s, Latin America grew rapidly for two reasons: international commodity prices were favorable, and interest rates were low. Countries could borrow at low rates with reasonable prospects of repayment. But in the early 1980s, interest rates rose sharply and remained elevated until early 1986. Commodity prices fell. Loans became more difficult to service, and the means to repay them diminished. As lenders became increasingly reluctant to extend additional credit, capital flows reversed, and Latin America actually lost resources. Both public and private spending fell as austerity programs took hold. Governments hard pressed to meet the commitments they had undertaken resorted to inflation as a means of finance; so although production fell, prices rose. As unemployment rose, wage payments fell, so that the gap between rich and poor widened. In short, during the 1980s, countries that felt the full impact of the debt crisis faced rising inflation and unemployment, increased poverty and social dislocation, falling living standards, greater inequality, and heightened social and political tensions. A Lost Decade indeed. At the same time, the stability of banks in the developed world, and particularly those in the United States, which had lent heavily to governments in Latin America, was threatened. As a result, the potential for a worldwide financial crisis loomed large, particularly in the early years of the 1980s.

The readings that follow consider the origins, consequences, and lessons of the crisis of the 1980s. Anne Krueger takes a regional view of the origins of the Latin American crisis, but also considers the ways in which the circumstances of particular borrowers came into play. Sebastian Edwards analyzes the reforms that borrowers were compelled to undertake, but he warns, in essence, that open economies and freer trade are not enough.

Origins of the Debt Crisis, 1970–1982

ANNE O. KRUEGER

Anne O. Krueger here provides a straightforward overview of the debt crisis that began in 1982. She suggests that though the developing countries faced a common problem, the circumstances of each borrower were different. In Mexico, which had become an oil exporter in the 1970s, the crisis was triggered in 1982 largely by a sharp decline in the price of crude oil. The decline was significant because Mexican borrowings in the international market were based on relatively optimistic assumptions about the price of crude oil.

Elsewhere, different circumstances intervened. Many countries that had turned in strong economic performances in the 1960s and 1970s slumped badly during the 1980s. In general, for-

Anne O. Krueger, "Origins of the Developing Countries' Debt Crisis, 1970–1982," *Journal of Development Economics,* 27 1 & 2 (1987), 165–170, 176, 178–186. Reprinted by permission of Elsevier Science B. V., Amsterdam, The Netherlands.

eign borrowing in Latin America had been a means of financing external deficits. But in some instances, notably in Argentina, Mexico, and Venezuela, foreign borrowing financed capital flight. For Central America, on the other hand, the principal source of poor economic performance in the early 1980s was unfavorable changes in international prices, for the economies of that region are small and quite open. For Argentina, Bolivia, and Venezuela, rising international interest rates, driven by economic policies in the United States, were the most serious concern. In still other places, such as Paraguay or Chile, economic performance suffered little (or much less) because of the debt crisis.

In the final analysis, resolving the debt crisis depended on a number of measures. Domestic reforms in the debtor nations were important, although the reduction in consumption that accompanied them produced a painful reduction in economic growth. Debt relief, in the form of the Baker Plan (1985), rescheduled payments and made their terms less onerous. The Brady Plan (1989) was quite important in that it proposed actual debt reduction. And finally, a sharp reduction in international lending rates, from over 16 percent in 1981 to 3 percent in 1994, was a major factor in resolving the Latin American debt crisis.

Anne O. Krueger is the author of *Political Economy of Policy Reform in Developing Countries* (1993), *Economic Policy Reform in Developing Countries* (1992), and *Perspectives on Trade and Development* (1990), among other works.

One of the most publicized features of the worldwide recession of 1980–83 was the 'debt crisis' of the developing countries. Within a short period of time, a number of developing countries switched from being sought-after and prized borrowers to uncreditworthy supplicants for rescheduling.

Until these events, conventional wisdom had been that the increasing ability of developing countries to get access to private international capital markets was a healthy development in the international economy. Capital-poor developing countries, so the reasoning went, had relatively high marginal products of capital and low savings rates, whereas rich countries had relatively lower marginal products of capital and higher savings rates; a flow of investible resources from rich to poor countries therefore appeared to be economically efficient, as well as desirable on humanitarian grounds. . . .

With high-return investments and rapid growth, most of those countries were well able to service their debts and established excellent reputations as borrowers. To be sure, individual countries had encountered debt-servicing difficulties: the Paris Club was formed in 1956 to reschedule Argentina's debt, and met periodically after that when particular countries found themselves unable to sustain scheduled debt-servicing obligations. Although developing countries as a group continued to rely primarily on official flows, a few shifted markedly toward the private international capital markets, and others began to borrow.

By 1970, it is estimated that developing countries as a group had a debt-service ratio of 14.7 percent, and that 50.9 percent of their debt was private, although the variation among groups of developing countries was enormous. For example, only 7 percent of low-income Asia's debt and 33.5 percent of low-income Africa's debt was private, and debt-service ratios ranged from 6.1 percent in Africa to 18.1 percent for middle income oil exporters.

When the price of oil quadrupled in 1973–74, the oil exporting countries had large current account surpluses. At first they placed their receipts largely in short-term deposits in commercial banks in the major financial centers. While the major oil importing developed countries incurred large current account deficits in 1974 and 1975, their current account positions were relatively rapidly restored. For the oil-importing developing countries, however, deficits were of longer duration, and financing by commercial banks rose sharply. The surpluses of the oil exporting countries were in effect 'recycled' through the commercial banks to the oil-importing developing countries.

Thus, during the 1973–80 period, developing countries' long-term debt outstanding and disbursed grew at an average annual rate of 21.3 percent, with private debt growing by 24 percent annually and official debt growing by 17.6 percent. Several factors, however, 'validated' this performance: (i) between 1973 and 1980, developing countries' export prices increased at an average annual rate of 14.7 percent; (ii) over the same period, the volume of exports from developing countries increased at an average annual rate of 4.1 percent; (iii) the interest rates charged on new public debt averaged 7 percent in 1974, 6.8 percent in 1976, and 7.9 percent in 1978; 23 percent of debt was at floating interest rates in 1976, 27 percent in 1978, and 32 percent in 1979.

As a consequence of rapid growth in export earnings, higher-than-anticipated inflation, and low nominal interest charges, the developing countries' debt-service ratios grew little during the 1970s. In 1978, the debt-service ratio for all developing countries stood at 18.4 percent (compared to 14.7 percent in 1970), and it fell to 16 percent by 1980. The developing countries' ratio of debt to exports was actually lower in 1980 than in 1970 — debt was 109 percent of exports in 1970 and 90 percent of exports in 1980! Thus, although nominal debt grew almost five-fold between 1970 and 1980, the developing countries' growth and export performance, worldwide inflation, and negative real interest rates obscured the imminent emergence of difficulties.

However, again there were significant differences between countries. Some developing countries encountered debt-servicing difficulties at various times in the 1970s: Argentina rescheduled in 1976, Peru in 1978, Turkey in 1978, 1979 and 1980, to name just a few. Although aggregate debt indicators were acceptable, there were individual countries with unsatisfactory and unsustainable balance of payments positions where significant policy reforms were needed, along with debt rescheduling, to prevent further economic difficulties. This experience is significant both in pointing to the fact that debt-servicing difficulties were not a new phenomenon in the 1980s, and in creating problems for estimation of the relative contributions of different factors to debt difficulties. . . .

To summarize: although some observers pointed with alarm to the rapid rate of increase in developing countries' debt after the oil price increase, most analysts regarded the increasing access to the private international financial market during that era as a symptom of the successful growth of those countries. Although individual countries encountered debt-servicing difficulties, the combination of a favorable world environment, relatively rapid growth of developing countries' exports, and worldwide inflation with negative real interest rates, all served to make the borrowing pattern seem sustainable.

Events of 1979–82 changed all that. With the second oil price increase, the OECD countries by and large adopted anti-inflationary macroeconomic policy stances. The result was severe worldwide recession, sharply falling commodity prices, and the highest real rates of interest in the post-war era. As contrasted with an average annual rate of increase of export unit values of 13.9 percent in the 1970–80 decade for the world as a whole, export unit values actually fell at an average annual rate of 3.3 percent during the 1980–83 period. The nominal value of world trade grew at an average annual rate of 20.1 percent during the 1970–80 decade (and at a rate of 15.5 percent even after 1974); from 1980 to 1983 it fell at an average rate of 1 percent.

Simultaneously, the average interest rates paid on new commitments rose from 7.9 percent in 1978 to a peak of 11.4 percent in 1981; for borrowers relying heavily on the private international capital market, the jump was even sharper. For Brazil, for instance, the rate was 9.9 percent in 1978 and 15.3 percent in 1981. For all developing countries, interest payments on total long-term debt outstanding rose from $16.8 billion in 1978 to $48 billion by 1982, a sharp jump indeed.

All countries felt the impact of the worldwide recession of 1980–83. All significant borrowers had difficulties with debt-servicing, and rates of real GNP growth fell almost everywhere. Some countries, including the Far Eastern exporters, Turkey (where debt difficulties had become pressing in 1979–80 but where policy reforms were so successful that creditworthiness was restored during the recession), and Colombia, avoided rescheduling and were able to maintain normal relations with their creditors. However, the vast majority of borrowers was unable to do so. And, even for most of the countries that maintained their access to credit markets, there were several years of significant adjustment and slower growth. . . .

As can be seen, the experience of the 1970s differed markedly among countries. Argentina, for example, restrained borrowing (and had a low rate of economic growth), and so was able to reduce the debt-export ratio despite a trade performance that was not quite average over the decade. Bolivia, Chile (probably because of copper), Jamaica, Peru, Uruguay and Venezuela experienced much lower growth of export earnings than corresponded to their trade-weighted share of the world fuel and non-fuel markets. A number of other countries also had below-average growth of exports, but by 2 percent annually or less. By contrast, Korea's exports grew much more rapidly than did world trade, and Brazil, Ecuador, Mexico and Nigeria (these latter two with rapidly rising shares of the world petroleum market) experienced increases in their market shares.

Turning then to the excess of the rate of growth of debt over exports: Brazil, Costa Rica, the Ivory Coast, Jamaica, Morocco,

Turkey, Venezuela and Yugoslavia had macroeconomic policies that led to a rate of borrowing significantly in excess of that which was sustainable on the basis of their export performance. Although Korea's debt grew rapidly, rapid export growth (with a rising market share) was more than enough to compensate for additional borrowing. A number of countries managed one way or another to limit the rate of increase of their debt to sustainable proportions: Bolivia, the Philippines and Uruguay are notable in that regard. Even Mexico, with a rapid rate of growth of export earnings, did not increase its debt as much: there was a very high debt-exports ratio to begin with which was sustainable only as long as exports could grow at an annual rate of 25 percent. By contrast, Argentina, Colombia, Korea and Nigeria had borrowed at less than sustainable rates, so that their debt-exports ratios had been declining in the 1970s. . . .

Thus, at the outset of the worldwide recession and disinflation which started in 1980, the initial situations of the countries covered here were vastly different. Some were experiencing satisfactory growth, apparently sustainable borrowing, and had relatively low debt/exports ratios. As such, they were apparently in excellent shape to withstand the turbulence of the early 1980s. At the other extreme were the countries where unsustainable growth of debt had persisted long enough so that the debt/exports ratios had reached levels which would in any event have presented major problems. In between were the countries with high rates of growth of debt but where policies had not persisted so long as to lead to excessive debt levels, given the conditions of the 1970s, and countries with high debt but apparently satisfactory prospects for export growth.

The new element introduced in the 1980s was the anti-inflationary macroeconomic policy stance adopted by the industrial countries. The 1970s were an inflationary period in which the real rate of interest was negative for several years. There were even some years in which developing countries' real debt outstanding declined despite significant new borrowing. While a prescient observer might have concluded that these conditions would not last forever, the shift in the 1980s was surely an 'unanticipated shock' which required significant adjustments. . . .

A factor of significance which has not been analyzed herein was the role of capital flight in the debt-servicing problems of the early 1980s. Capital flight itself is often symptomatic of underlying macroeconomic or trade-regime problems, and hence cannot be considered independently of other contributory factors. Insofar as capital flight is an 'expectations variable', it would be triggered by such phenomena as relatively low growth rates of exports relative to debt, which in turn could result either directly from expansionary macroeconomic policies or from efforts to maintain nominal exchange rates in the face of domestic inflation.

Nonetheless, even the crude quantification points clearly to the extreme diversity among developing countries in initial situations and in responses to the changed world conditions of the 1980s. Recognition of this diversity is important for understanding the present positions of many developing countries, but it is only a first step. Whether the debt difficulties of a country were the result of the changed world environment or of inappropriate domestic policies is not the end of the story: either way, economic policies and incentives require realignment to encourage efficient resource allocation, accumulation and growth.

The Results of Trade Reform

SEBASTIAN EDWARDS

In this excerpt, Sebastian Edwards looks at developments since the 1980s, and in particular, surveys the market-oriented reforms in Latin America inspired by the debt crisis. As Lustig, Maddison, Ranis, Thorp and others suggest, between the 1930s and the 1980s, Latin America turned away from the international economy, not only following unorthodox policies but developing distinctively heterodox ideologies to justify them. Edwards indicates that since the 1980s, the return to orthodoxy has been striking. For example, the reduction of tariffs and nontariff barriers to trade since the 1980s has been substantial, and in Brazil, Colombia, Mexico, Paraguay, and Peru the change has been nothing short of spectacular.

Sebastian Edwards, "Trade Liberalization Reforms in Latin America: Recent Experiences, Policy Issues and Further Prospects," in Graham Bird and Ann Helwege, eds., *Latin America's Economic Future* (San Diego: Academic Press, 1994), pp. 14–17, 27–28, 31–32, 42–44. Reprinted by permission of Academic Press.

Edwards suggests that stronger links to the international market offer a variety of benefits, not least of which are major gains in productive efficiency. He argues that almost everywhere in Latin America, with the possible exception of Mexico, open economies and productivity increase have gone hand-in-hand. Economists like Robert Lucas argue that export markets, which are by definition larger and more competitive than the home market, increase the appeal of adopting technologically sophisticated methods of production. These techniques inevitably spill over into the home market, as workers trained in the export sector bring new skills to bear on domestic production as well. Imported capital goods also bring access to newer technologies, while competition from imports gives producers incentives to adopt more efficient techniques.

Nevertheless, Edwards argues that openness is not enough. Countries that seek to gain from liberalized foreign trade regimes need to maintain realistic, competitive exchange rates. Edwards warns that fixed exchange rates pose potential dangers, for if domestic prices rise, the balance of trade will deteriorate as the home currency becomes overvalued and imports increase. If foreign investors (or currency speculators) doubt the willingness or ability of a government to defend a fixed exchange rate, a financial crisis may ensue as investors panic and sell off their assets. The financial crisis can easily spread to the real economy as consumption, investment, and production fall. In the face of massive layoffs, falling consumption, rising interest rates and inflation, and bank failures, a government's ability (or political will) to sustain reform and liberalization may falter and even be destroyed. Although Edwards was writing with the experience of Chile in 1979–1982 in mind, his conclusion, "What Does All of This Mean for Mexico?" turned out to be all too relevant. In the wake of an ill-managed devaluation of the Mexican peso in December 1994, private economists predicted a fall in Mexican GDP of at least 4.8 percent in 1995, along with unprecedented declines in private consumption and investment. As the *Financial Times* pointed out in an editorial "Lessons from Mexico's Crisis," April 7, 1995, "[O]pen economies enjoy a very narrow margin of manoeuver. . . . The combination of an overvalued exchange rate with undue credit expansion, a run-down in foreign exchange reserves and excessive reliance on short-term borrowing was the proximate cause of Mexico's crisis." Another prescient view of the Mexican situation appeared in Rudiger Dornbusch, "Mexico: How to Recover Stability and Growth" in his *Stabilization, Debt, and Reform* (1993).

Sebastian Edwards is the author of *Reform, Recovery and Growth: Latin America and the Middle East* (1995) and coeditor of *The Macroeconomics of Populism in Latin America* (1991, with Rudiger Dornbusch), *Real Exchange Rates, Devaluation and Adjustment* (1989), and numerous other major publications.

The Economic Consequences of Protectionism

Latin America's long tradition of protectionist policies moulded the region's economic structure in a fundamental way. Perhaps the most important consequence of protectionism was that, from early on, high import tariffs and prohibitions generated a severe anti-export bias that discouraged both the growth and diversification of exports. In an early study using data from the 1960s, Bela Balassa (1971) found that the Latin American countries in his sample — Brazil, Chile and Mexico — had some of the most distorted foreign trade patterns in the world. These findings coincided with those obtained by Little *et al.* in their pioneer study on trade policy and industrialization in the developing world. These authors persuasively argued that the high degree of protection granted to manufacturing in Latin America resulted in a serious discrimination against exports, in resource misallocation, inefficient investment and deteriorating income distribution. They further argued that the reversal of the protectionist policies should be at the centre of any reformulation of Latin America's development strategy. However, at the time these proposals were being made, Latin America was still moving strongly in the opposite direction, pushing protectionist policies to a global level through the formation of custom unions with high common external tariffs.

The discouragement of exports activities took place through two main channels: first, import tariffs, quotas and prohibitions increased the cost of imported intermediate materials and capital goods used in the production of exportables, reducing their effective rate of protection. In fact, for years a vast number of exportable goods, especially those in the agricultural sector, had *negative* rates protection to their value added. Second, and perhaps more important, the maze of protectionist policies resulted in real exchange rate overvaluation that reduced the degree of competitiveness of exports. This anti-export bias explains the poor performance of the export sector, including the inability to aggressively develop non-traditional exports, during the twenty years preceding the debt crisis. Paradoxically, policies which were supposed to reduce Latin America's dependence on the world-wide business cycle, ended up creating a highly vulnerable economic structure where the sources of foreign exchange were concentrated on a few products intensive in natural resources.

A second important consequence of traditional protective trade policies was the creation of an inefficient manufacturing sector. Instead of granting short-term protection to help launch new activities, high tariffs, quotas and prohibitions became a fixture of the region's economic landscape. What originally were thought to be cases for temporary import protection — based on infant industry arguments — rapidly required permanent protective assistance in order to survive. Rapidly, the system generated a large number of lobbyists that constantly argued for privileged treatment for their particular industries. It is not an exaggeration to say that in many countries, being able to obtain special treatment on protective matters became more important than increasing productivity, developing new products, or implementing technological innovations. As a result of all this, in most Latin American countries the rate of growth of productivity was very low during the imports-substitution epoch.

An important consequence of the pressures exercised by lobbyists and interest groups was that the protective structure in Latin America became extremely uneven, with some sectors enjoying effective tariff rates in the thousands, and others suffering from negative value added protection.

The ECLA-supported policies also had serious effects on labour markets. In particular, the protection of capital-intensive industries affected the region's ability to create employment. A number of studies have shown that more open trade regimes in the developing countries have resulted in higher employment and in a more even income distribution than protectionist regimes. For example, after analysing in detail the experiences of ten countries, Krueger (1983) concluded that exportable industries tended to be significantly more labour-intensive than import-competing sectors. In the conclusions to this massive study, Krueger argues that employment has tended to grow faster in outward-oriented economies, and that the removal of external sector distortions will tend to help the employment creation process in most developing nations. These results were broadly supported by other cross-country studies, including Balassa and Michaely *et al.* . . .

To sum up, although several decades of protectionist policies accomplished the goal of creating an industrial sector in Latin America, this was achieved at a high cost. Exports were severely discouraged, the exchange rate became overvalued, employment creation lagged and massive amounts of resources—including skilled human talent—were withdrawn from the productive sphere and devoted to lobbying for ever-increasingly favourable treatment of different sectors of the economy. An increasing number of comparative studies in the 1970s and 1980s made the shortcomings of the Latin American development strategies particularly apparent. In the aftermath of the debt crisis the long stagnation, and even regression, of the region's export sector—which experienced an average rate of decline of 1 per cent a year between 1965 and 1980—became particularly painful to the local public, analysts and policymakers. . . .

Trade Liberalization and Productivity Growth

The relaxation of trade impediments has had a fundamental impact on the region's economies. Suddenly, Latin America's industry, which to a large extent had developed and grown behind protective walls, was forced to compete. Many firms have not been able to survive this shock, and have become bankrupt. Others, however, have faced the challenge of lower protection by embarking on major restructuring, and increasing their level of productivity.

The ability (and willingness) of firms to implement significant adjustment depend on two main factors: the degree of credibility of the reform, and the level of distortions in the labour market. If entrepreneurs believe that the reform will not persist through time, there will be no incentive to incur the costs of adjusting the product mix and of increasing the degree of productive efficiency. In fact, if the reform is perceived as temporary, the optimal behaviour is not to adjust; instead it is profitable to speculate through the accumulation of imported durable goods. This was, as Rodriguez has documented, the case in Argentina during the failed reforms of Martinez de Hoz.

In their studies on the interaction between labour markets and structural reforms Krueger and Michaely *et al.* found that most successful trade reforms have indeed resulted in major increases in labour productivity. In most cases where this has happened, labour markets have been characterized by some degree of flexibility. Countries with rigid and highly distorted labour markets — including countries with high costs of dismissal, limitations on temporary contracts and rigid minimum wage legislation — have generally exhibited modest improvements in labour productivity after the reform process.

Some of the early Latin American reformers have experienced important labour productivity improvements. For example, according to Edwards and Cox-Edwards, labour productivity in the Chilean manufacturing sector increased at an average annual rate of 13.4 per cent between 1978 and 1981. On the other hand, the available evidence suggests that the increase in labour productivity in the Mexican manufacturing sector in the post-reform period has been more moderate. According to Sánchez, labour productivity in Mexico's manufacturing sector increased at an annual rate of 3.8 per cent between 1986 and 1991. Still, this figure is more than double the historical annual rate of growth of labour productivity in the manufacturing sector between 1960 and 1982 — 1.6 per cent.

As discussed above, recent models of growth have suggested that countries that are more open to the rest of the world will exhibit a faster rate of technological improvement and productivity growth than countries that isolate themselves from the rest of the world. From an empirical point of view, this means that countries that open up their external sectors, and engage in trade liberalization reforms, will experience an *increase* in total factor productivity growth, relative to the pre-reform period. . . .

The volume of international trade in Latin America, and in particular the volume of exports, increased significantly after the reforms were initiated. For example, while for the region as a whole the volume of exports grew at an annual rate of only 2.0 per cent between 1970 and 1980, it grew at a rate of 5.5 per cent between 1980 and 1985, and at an annual average of 6.7 per cent between 1986 and 1990. Although, strictly speaking, it is not possible to fully attribute this export surge to the opening-up reforms, there is significant country-specific evidence suggesting that a more open economy, and in particular a more depreciated real exchange rate, has positively affected exports growth. Some countries, especially Costa Rica, have accompanied the opening-up process with the implementation of a battery of export promotion schemes, including tax credits — through the "Certificado de Abono Tributario" — duty free imports and income tax exemptions. However, some authors, including Nogues and Gulati, have argued that these systems have not been an effective way of encouraging exports. . . .

What Does All of This Mean for Mexico?

The analysis presented above has documented the dramatic change in foreign trade policy in Latin America during the last few years. The region, which for many decades had followed strict protectionist policies, has opened up significantly to the rest of the world. Tariffs have been slashed, NTBs have been eliminated in many countries and the dispersion of protective measures has been greatly reduced. The purpose of these policies has been threefold: first, by eliminating distortions, it is expected that resources will be allocated in a more efficient way, reducing the waste that for many years plagued the region. Second, lower protectionism is expected to reduce the traditional anti-export bias, encouraging exports growth and diversification. And third, the trade reforms are expected to increase productivity growth and help modernize the region. This, in turn, will help improve income distribution over the longer run.

The data analysis presented above shows that, in general, trade reforms in Latin America have helped expand exports and increase productivity growth. This has particularly been the case for Chile, the pioneer Latin American reformer. What is surprising, however, is that our analysis shows that in Mexico, another of the early reformers, the expected positive effects of the reforms have not materialized fully. In fact, comparisons between the Chilean and Mexican cases shows an important difference in export growth and diversification, and productivity improvements. Moreover, when other elements are brought into the analysis — including real wage performance, trade balance evolution and overall real GDP growth — the contrast between the two countries is even more marked.

There are several possible explanations for the performance of the Mexican economy and, in particular, for its contrast with the case of Chile. First, the Chilean reforms have been in place for a much longer period of time — roughly since 1976–7. Second, in Chile the reforms were credible from early on, and towards the late

1970s investment in export-oriented sectors began to boom. Ibarra (1992) has argued that this has not been the case in Mexico. In fact, he documents a very low level of new investment in those sectors with greater comparative advantage. This could reflect the uncertainty introduced by NAFTA into the future of Mexico's trade policy. Investors decided to "wait and see" whether NAFTA was actually implemented before committing themselves to major projects. And third, the fact that in Chile the reforms were broad, affecting many sectors which reinforced each other, contrasts with the piecemeal approach followed by Mexico.

An analysis of the "determinants" of successful trade reforms shows that, in the case of Mexico, some of these requirements have not been met:

1. Although non-traditional exports have grown rapidly, the actual rate of expansion has not been as spectacular as in Chile and Costa Rica. In fact, after expanding fast in 1983–7, non-oil exports as a percentage of GDP seem to have levelled off at around 6.7 per cent.
2. As was shown above, aggregate factor productivity growth in Mexico has not increased in the post-reform period. And the rate of acceleration of productivity growth in manufacturing, although positive, has been only modest.
3. A positive factor is that unemployment has stayed low — below 3 per cent in the last few years. Additionally, the *Programa de Solidaridad Social* has provided an effective safety net for the poorer segment of society. As a result of this, the transformation of the economy has not been associated with employment dislocations.
4. Real wages, however, have stayed practically stagnant in the economy as a whole, as well as in manufacturing. This, of course, is the reflection of the slow growth in productivity.
5. The trade balance has become increasingly negative. This has been possible thanks to the large inflow of foreign capital experienced in the last few years, which has allowed the country to finance the widening gap between imports and exports. There is, however, a clear danger that the public might perceive this large trade deficit as unsustainable in the medium run. This may indeed lead to a loss of credibility in the programme as a whole. The rapid real appreciation experienced by the peso in

the last few years has contributed to this widening trade imbalance, affecting overall credibility.

In many ways, the picture described above does not conform with the successful and sustained liberalizations identified in the economics literature. In fact, under "normal" conditions, analysts could be tempted to argue that Mexico's reform would not be long-lived and, under heavy political pressure, would be reversed. However, Mexico is not a "normal" case. It is politically unique and, by promoting NAFTA, the Mexican authorities have been able to provide credibility to the trade reform programme. In particular, by legally tying the government's hands, the approval of NAFTA indicates that, even if the programme has not borne fruits (yet), there will be no turning back towards protectionism and isolationism. By signing NAFTA, the Mexican government has effectively bought credibility, and hopes to greatly reduce the degree of speculation on the possible reversibility of the reforms. In other words, the Mexican government has obtained additional time to show that trade liberalization indeed works and is the appropriate route for the new century.

SUGGESTIONS FOR FURTHER READING

Dependency and world-systems theory have had a significant impact on the study of Latin America and the world economy. A full bibliography would be impossible here; I mention only several of the more influential or recent works in English, and foreign-language titles for which there are no close English-language substitutes. A particularly good introduction to the large and complex literature is Cristóbal Kay, *Latin American Theories of Development and Underdevelopment* (London: Routledge, 1989). For a pithy discussion see J. G. Palma, "Dependency," in John Eatwell, Murray Milgate, and Peter Newman, eds., *The New Palgrave: A Dictionary of Economics* (London: The Macmillan Press, 1987), 1:802–805. Ian Roxborough, *Theories of Underdevelopment* (Atlantic Highlands, N.J.: Humanities Press, 1979) remains useful. For a dissenter's view, see Robert Packenham, *The Dependency Movement: Scholarship and Politics in Development Studies* (Cambridge: Harvard University Press, 1992). Stephen Haggard, *Pathways from the Periphery: The Politics of Growth in the Newly Industrializing Countries* (Ithaca, N.Y.: Cornell University Press, 1990) examines the dependency question from the perspective of comparative politics in East Asia and Latin America. A formal economic treatment of these issues appears in Edmar Bacha, "An Interpretation of Unequal Exchange from Prebisch-Singer to Emmanuel," *Journal of Development Economics* 5 (1978): 319–330. But also see Dimitris Diakosavvas and Pasquale L. Scandizzo, "Trends in the Terms of Primary Commodities, 1900–1982: The Controversy and Its Origins," *Economic Development and Cultural Change* 39, no. 2 (1991): 231–264, which contains a valuable bibliographical appendix.

Historians of the Spanish and Portuguese empires have been deeply influenced by the literature on dependency and world systems. A classic expression of the dependency school is Stanley J. and Barbara H. Stein, *The Colonial Heritage of Latin America: Essays on Economic Dependence in Perspective* (New York: Oxford University Press, 1970). The Steins' work was itself placed in perspective in the early 1980s by Tulio Halperín Donghi; see his "Dependency Theory and Latin American Historiography," *Latin American Research Review* 17, no. 1 (1982): 115–130, as well as related papers on dependency and world-system thinking in the same issue. Another starting point is Andre Gunder Frank's *Capitalism and Underdevelopment in Latin America: Historical Studies of Chile and Brazil* (New York: Monthly Review Press, 1967). Steve J. Stern's "Feudalism, Capitalism, and the World-System in the Perspective of Latin America and the Caribbean," *American Historical Review* 93, no. 4 (1988): 829–872, places the work of Immanuel Wallerstein in a Latin American perspective and offers an ample review of the relevant scholarship. Carl Hanson's "The European 'Renovation' and Luso-Atlantic Economy, 1560–1715," *Review* 6, no. 4 (1983): 475–530, applies Wallerstein's ideas to Luso-Brazilian studies and has an extensive bibliography. Leandro Prados de la Escosura and Jorge-Miguel Pedreira have attempted to measure the effects of the loss of Spain and Portugal's American colonies on the metropolitan economies; see their chapters in Leandro Prados and Samuel Amaral, eds., *La independencia americana: consecuencias económicas* (Madrid: Alianza Editorial, 1993).

The appearance of Victor Bulmer-Thomas's *The Economic History of Latin America Since Independence* (Cambridge: Cambridge University Press, 1994) provides the first comprehensive study of Latin America in the international economy since independence. Indeed, Bulmer-Thomas argues that the mechanics of export-led growth constitute what the late Frank Tannenbaum termed a "key"—one of three, in Bulmer-Thomas's view—to understanding Latin American economic development. Writings on the nineteenth century in general grow rapidly. For a general survey that incorporates some international materials, see William Glade, "Economy, 1870–1914," in Leslie Bethell, ed., *Latin America: Economy and Society, 1870–1930* (Cambridge: Cambridge University Press, 1989). Three key collections of papers that touch on Latin America and the world economy appeared in the 1980s. Roberto Cortés Conde and Shane J. Hunt, eds., *The Latin American Economies: Growth and the Export Sector, 1880–1930* (New York: Holmes and Meier, 1985) deals explicitly with the issues raised here. So too does *Guiding the Invisible Hand: Economic Liberalism and the State in Latin American History* (New York: Praeger, 1988), edited by Joseph L. Love and Nils Jacobsen. A third, wide-ranging collection representing international political economy is Christopher Abel and Colin M. Lewis, eds., *Latin America, Economic Imperialism, and the State: The Political Economy of the External Connection from Independence to the Present* (London: Athlone, 1985).

A number of essential country studies overlap the nineteenth and twentieth centuries. For Argentina through the fall of Rosas and somewhat beyond, see Jonathan C. Brown, *A Socioeconomic History of Argentina, 1776–1860* (Cambridge: Cambridge University Press, 1979). For the period beginning in 1860, see Carlos Díaz Alejandro, *Essays on the Economic History of the Argentine Republic* (New Haven: Yale University Press, 1970), as well as Díaz Alejandro's "No Less Than One Hundred Years of Argentine Economic History Plus Some Comparisons," in Andrés Velasco, ed., *Trade, Development, and the World Economy: Selected Essays of Carlos F. Díaz Alejandro* (Oxford: Basil Blackwell, 1988).

On Brazil, see Nathaniel Leff, *Underdevelopment and Development in Brazil*, 2 vols. (Boston: Allen & Unwin, 1982); Carlos Manuel Peláez, "The Theory and Reality of Imperialism in the Coffee Economy of Nineteenth-Century Brazil," *The Economic History Review*, 2d ser., 29, no. 2 (1976): 276–290; and more recently, Eugene Ridings, *Business Groups in Nineteenth-Century Brazil* (Cambridge: Cambridge University Press, 1994). Winston Fritsch, *External Constraints on Economic Policy in Brazil, 1889–1930* (Pittsburgh: University of Pittsburgh Press, 1988) deals mainly with the years between 1914 and 1930, focusing on the gold standard, monetary policy, levels of state autonomy, and more. Steven Topik, *The Political Economy of the Brazilian State, 1889–1930* (Austin: University of Texas Press, 1900) is a valuable contribution as well.

On Central America, see Victor Bulmer-Thomas, *The Political Economy of Central America Since 1920* (Cambridge: Cambridge University Press, 1987), a critical examination of export-led growth in Central America; as well as his *Studies in the Economics of Central America* (New York: St. Martin's Press, 1988), especially Part I, "Long-Run Studies." Robert G. Williams, *Export Agriculture and the Crisis in Central America* (Chapel Hill: University of North Carolina Press, 1986) focuses on the cotton and beef export booms.

For Chile, Markos J. Mamalakis, *The Growth and Structure of the Chilean Economy: From Independence to Allende* (New Haven: Yale University Press, 1976) is essential. Sebastian Edwards and Alejandra Cox Edwards, in *Monetarism and Liberalization: The Chilean Experiment* (Cambridge, Mass.: Ballinger, 1987), deals with recent events, as does Barry P. Bosworth, Rudiger Dornbusch, and Raúl Labán, eds., *The Chilean Economy: Policy Lessons and Challenges* (Washington, D.C.: The Brookings Institute, 1994).

On Colombia, see William Paul McGreevey, *An Economic History of Colombia, 1845–1930* (Cambridge: Cambridge University Press, 1971) and Marco Palacios, *Coffee in Colombia, 1850–1970* (Cambridge: Cambridge University Press, 1980), as well as Carlos F. Díaz Alejandro, *Foreign Trade Regimes and Economic Development: Colombia* (New York: NBER and Columbia University Press, 1976). Also see Jon V. Kofas, *Dependence and Underdevelopment in Colombia* (Tempe: Arizona State University, Center for Latin American Studies, 1986).

For Mexico, Fernando Rosenzweig Hernández, *El desarrollo económico de México: 1800–1910* (Toluca, 1989) is basic. A paper that characterizes dependency, monopoly, and exploitation as evocative terms is Fred Carstensen and Diane Roazen, "Foreign Markets, Domestic Initiative, and the Emergence of a Monocrop Economy: The Yucatecan Experience, 1825–1903," *HAHR* 72, no. 4 (1992): 555–592. The standard modern account is Clark Winton Reynolds, *The Mexican Economy: Twentieth Century Structure and Growth* (New Haven: Yale University Press, 1970), but see also René Villareal, *El desequilibrio externo en la industrialización de México (1929–1975): Un enfoque estructuralista* (Mexico City: Fondo de Cultura Económica, 1976) and Enrique Cárdenas, *La industrialización mexicana durante la Gran Depresión* (Mexico City: El Colegio de México, 1978).

There is no better work on early national Peru than Paul Gootenberg's *Between Silver and Guano: Commercial Policy and the State in Postindependence Peru* (Princeton: Princeton University Press, 1989). But see also Gootenberg's important "Carneros y chuño: Price Levels in Nineteenth-Century Peru," *Hispanic American Historical Review* 70, no. 1 (1990): 1–56. The story is taken up after the War of the Pacific in Rosemary Thorp and Geoffrey Bertram, *Peru 1890–1977: Growth and Policy in an Open Economy* (New York: Columbia University Press, 1978). Thorp updates this history in "Trends and Cycles in the Peruvian Economy," *Journal of Development Economics* 27 (1987): 356–374. More recent developments are discussed in Carlos E. Paredes and Jeffrey Sachs, eds., *Peru's Path to Recovery: A Plan for Economic Stabilization and Growth* (Washington, D.C.: The Brookings Institute, 1991).

For Latin American foreign economic relations with Great Britain in the nineteenth (and twentieth) centuries, see Rory Miller, *Britain and Latin America in the Nineteenth and Twentieth Centuries* (London: Longman, 1993). But see also P. J. Cain and A. G. Hopkins, *British Imperialism: Innovation and Expansion, 1688–1914* (London: Longman, 1993), in particular Chapter 9, "Calling the New World into Existence: South America, 1815–1914," For British lending to Latin America, see Lance E. Davis and Robert J. Huttenback, *Mammon and the Pursuit of Empire: The Political Economy of British Imperialism, 1860–1912* (Cambridge: Cambridge University Press, 1986); and D. C. M. Platt, *Britain's Investment Overseas on the Eve of the First World War: The Use and Abuse of Numbers* (London: Macmillan, 1986). An interesting discussion of lending to Latin America by the British merchant bank Barings appears in Philip Ziegler, *The Sixth Great Power: A History of the House of Barings, 1762–1929* (New York: Alfred A. Knopf, 1988). For United States lending, see Lance E. Davis and Robert J. Cull, *International Capital Markets and American Economic Growth, 1820–1914* (Cambridge: Cambridge University Press, 1994) and Barbara Stallings, *Banker to the Third World: U.S. Portfolio Investment in Latin America, 1900–1986* (Berkeley: University of California Press, 1987).

In addition to the specific country studies just listed, there are a number of useful thematic volumes on the twentieth century. A general essay on the early twentieth century with much material on trade and finance is Rosemary Thorp, "Economy, 1914–1920," in Leslie Bethell, ed., *Latin America: Economy and Society, 1870–1930* (Cambridge: Cambridge University Press, 1989). A recent text with ample coverage of international issues is Eliana Cardoso and Ann Helwege, *Latin America's Economy: Di-*

versity, Trends, and Conflict (Cambridge: MIT Press, 1992). On the international economic impact of World War I, see Bill Albert (with the assistance of Paul Henderson), *South America and the First World War: The Impact of the War on Brazil, Argentina, Peru, and Chile* (Cambridge: Cambridge University Press, 1988). A preliminary summary of the book appeared in *World Development* 9, no. 8 (1981): 717–734. On Latin America and the Depression, see Rosemary Thorp, ed., *Latin America in the 1930s: The Role of the Periphery in World Crisis* (Oxford, U.K.: Macmillan Press, 1984), especially the essay by Carlos Díaz Alejandro. The 1940s has a historiography of its own; see David Rock, ed., *Latin America in the 1940s: War and Postwar Transitions* (Berkeley: University of California Press, 1994), with particular attention to the essay by Rosemary Thorp. Similarly, see Leslie Bethell and Ian Roxborough, eds., *Latin America Between the Second World War and the Cold War, 1944–1948* (Cambridge: Cambridge University Press, 1992). A series of contemporary studies on Argentina, Brazil, Chile, Colombia, Peru, and Uruguay appears in Demetris Papageorgiou, Michael Michaely, and Armeane M. Choksi, *Liberalizing Foreign Trade*, 7 vols. (Oxford, U.K: Basil Blackwell, 1991).

One of the best historical studies to emerge from the debt crisis of the 1980s is Carlos Marichal, *A Century of Debt Crises in Latin America: From Independence to the Great Depression, 1820–1930* (Princeton: Princeton University Press, 1989). An authoritative collection of papers that deals substantially with Latin America is Barry Eichengreen and Peter H. Lindert, eds., *The International Debt Crisis in Historical Perspective* (Cambridge: MIT Press, 1989). Rosemary Thorp and Laurence Whitehead, *Latin American Debt and the Adjustment Crisis* (Pittsburgh: University of Pittsburgh Press, 1987) is a valuable contribution to the literature as well. But see also David Felix, ed., *Debt and Transfiguration: Prospects for Latin America's Economic Revival* (Armonk, N.Y.: M. E. Sharpe, 1990).